Moses Harvey

Text-Book of Newfoundland History

Moses Harvey

Text-Book of Newfoundland History

ISBN/EAN: 9783337327545

Printed in Europe, USA, Canada, Australia, Japan

Cover: Foto ©Paul-Georg Meister /pixelio.de

More available books at **www.hansebooks.com**

TEXT-BOOK

OF

NEWFOUNDLAND HISTORY,

FOR THE

USE OF SCHOOLS AND ACADEMIES.

BY

THE REV. M. HARVEY,

Author of "*Newfoundland — the Oldest British Colony;*" "*Lectures, Literary and Biographical;*" Articles, "*Newfoundland*" and "*Labrador,*" in the *Encyclopædia Britannica*, etc.

With Map and Illustrations.

BOSTON:
DOYLE AND WHITTLE, PUBLISHERS
1885.

TO TEACHERS.

The author of this little work has aimed at narrating the leading events in the history of Newfoundland in such clear and simple language as may attract the attention of the young, and at the same time prove interesting to those of maturer years. While unecessary details have been avoided, no event of importance has been passed over.

The author would respectfully but earnestly point out to teachers who may use this volume, the great importance of connecting the geography of the narrative with the history, in order to fix the knowledge acquired permanently in the memory, and render it useful. The situation of every place mentioned in the history should be pointed out by the pupils on the map, and its position with reference to other places should be carefully learned. The place being thus associated with the event in the minds of the learners, both are more clearly realized and more deeply impressed on the memory. To aid teachers, and expedite their work, a series of questions on the history and on the geography of the places mentioned has been appended to each chapter.

A summary of the chronology of each period is also given, in which the dates of the most important events and of the more prominent personages are noted. This helps to give the pupil a connected view of history as a whole, and enables him to obtain some idea of contemporary events in other countries, and thus to link the records of his own land with those of the rest of the world. Thus the aids of geography and chronology impart a deeper interest to historical studies, and render their results more satisfactory and permanent.

CONTENTS.

	Page
CHAPTER I.	
First Discoveries	9
CHAPTER II.	
The Red Indians, or Aboriginal Inhabitants of Newfoundland	25
CHAPTER III.	
Exploration and Settlement of America . .	35
CHAPTER IV.	
England takes Possession of Newfoundland	42
CHAPTER V.	
The Fisheries	54
CHAPTER VI.	
Whitbourne's Commission . . .	61
CHAPTER VII.	
Contemporary Events	68
CHAPTER VIII.	
The French in Newfoundland	74
CHAPTER IX.	
Condition of the Early Settlers . . .	79
CHAPTER X.	
Renewed Efforts of the French to Conquer Newfoundland	90
CHAPTER XI.	
"The Seven Years' War"	98

		Page
CHAPTER XII.		
Palliser's Act	. . . .	108
CHAPTER XIII.		
Commercial Disasters	. . . .	124
CHAPTER XIV.		
Important Events	. . . .	149
CHAPTER XV.		
Conclusion	. . . .	164
Appendix	. . . .	175

LIST OF ILLUSTRATIONS.

	Page
City of St. John's	Frontispiece
Columbus	13
Sebastian Cabot	15
Amerigo Vespucci	17
Wigwam Point	31
Jacques Cartier	45
Sir Humphrey Gilbert	47
Sir Walter Raleigh	49
Sir Francis Drake	55
Lord Baltimore	63
Cecil, Second Lord Baltimore	65
Placentia	facing page 74
Bett's Cove Harbour	facing page 151
Government House, St. John's	157
Church of England Cathedral, St. John's . . .	165
Roman Catholic Cathedral, St. John's . .	167
Cochrane-street Methodist Church, St. John's .	169
St. Andrew's Presbyterian Church, St. John's .	171
Roman Catholic Cathedral, Harbour Grace .	173

INTRODUCTION.

At first sight it might be supposed that there was little worthy of attention in the history of Newfoundland. The general impression about it, till lately, has been that it is merely a barren, fog-enveloped island, where a few thousand fishermen secure a precarious existence by catching and curing the fish which abound in its waters. "What," it might be asked, "can there be worth knowing regarding their achievements? The tale must be barren and uninteresting."

I submit that this is a great mistake. The story of this colony connects itself with the history of both England and America, and presents points of the deepest interest. The first North American land which was discovered was the shores of this island. In the New World England's flag first floated here. Her first attempt at colonization was made here. Her first success in maritime discovery was won here. In prosecuting the fisheries of Newfoundland English sailors first learned how to rule the waves. The wealth derived from these fisheries added largely to England's greatness, and for many years these fisheries were the best nursery for her seamen. Great and heroic men took part in the early colonization of the island; and the glory which their names shed on its history should never be forgotten.

In later times the history of the island connected itself closely with that of the other British colonies of North America, and it had a share in the great conflicts which decided their destiny. On its shores a race of hardy, industrious men created a home for themselves, in spite of difficulties, opposition, and oppression. The battle of freedom was fought and won here by determined, much-enduring men, though it was a bloodless conflict. Through toils and sufferings of no ordinary severity the colony won its way to self-government, and the attainment of its constitutional rights and liberties.

The story of this ancient colony is, therefore, neither unimportant nor uninstructive. To its own people, in particular, a knowledge of the struggles and vicissitudes through which it has passed cannot fail to be of deep interest and importance.

This is especially true regarding the young, on whom the hopes of its future largely depend. They should be early familiarized with the history of their own country. Before they can love their country intelligently, and cherish that patriotic feeling which will lift them above mere party or selfish considerations, and enable them to feel an honest pride in their island-home, and to labour for its advancement, they must acquaint themselves with its history.

In this little volume I have endeavoured to present a brief historical sketch of Newfoundland, which may interest and inform the minds of the young, and be adapted for use in schools and academies; while it may also serve to impart a knowledge of the country's past to those of mature years who have not time for the study of larger works on the subject. No school history of Newfoundland has yet been published. It will be a source of gratification to me if I have succeeded in meeting a want which has long been felt, by supplying a history which teachers can use with advantage.

M. HARVEY.

St. John's, Newfoundland, ———, 1885.

HISTORY OF NEWFOUNDLAND.

CHAPTER I.

FROM 1001 TO 1498.

FIRST DISCOVERERS.

THE COMING OF THE NORTHMEN. — DISCOVERY OF THE NEW WORLD. — JOHN CABOT AND HIS SON SEBASTIAN.

1. A GLANCE at a map of North America shows us a large island, somewhat triangular in shape, lying right across the entrance of the Gulf of St. Lawrence, to which it affords access at its northern and southern extremities. This is the island of Newfoundland. It occupies an important position, being near the mainland of America, while its most eastern projection is but 1,640 miles from the western coast of Ireland. Its south-western extremity is within fifty miles of the Island of Cape Breton, and its northern point approaches within ten miles of the coast of Labrador. It thus forms, as it were, a stepping-stone between the Old World and the New. In regard to magnitude, it ranks tenth among the islands of the globe, its greatest length being 317 miles, its greatest breadth 316 miles, and its area 42,000 square miles. It is thus one-sixth larger than Ireland, and equal in area to two-thirds that of England and Wales. Its coast-line is 2,000 miles in extent.

2. It is curious to find that five hundred years before the days of Columbus and Cabot, the Northmen, or

Norsemen, as the inhabitants of Norway and Sweden were then called, had discovered Newfoundland, and visited and even colonized portions of the neighbouring mainland of America. These Northmen were, in the tenth and eleventh centuries, the greatest mariners of their time, and, like their descendants, the Norwegians, Swedes, and Danes, had a wonderful love for the sea and for maritime adventures. In their frail barks they pushed out into the northern seas, and discovered and colonized Iceland, about the year 870. Fifty or a hundred years afterwards they planted colonies on both the eastern and western shores of Greenland. It is not wonderful that, being so near the western coast of Davis Strait, they should have crossed over from Greenland in their numerous voyages; and, once there, it was an easy matter to trace the coast to Labrador, Newfoundland, and farther southward.

3. Thus there is nothing at all improbable in the story told in the Norse books, called Sagas, regarding the visits of these bold sailors to the coast of North America. The story is told in this way: About the year 1001, one of their ships, when on a voyage from Iceland to Greenland, was driven away far to the south-west by a tempest, and at length came in sight of a richly-wooded, level country. The wind abated, and the sailors shaped their course for Greenland. The news of their great discovery fired the heart of Leif, son of Eric the Red, who had founded the Greenland colony. He at once resolved to set out and explore the new country, of which he had received such a glowing account. He was accompanied on this voyage by Bjorn.

4. The bold adventurers first reached a rocky island, to which they gave the name of Helluland, or the land of naked rocks. This must have been Newfoundland, which lay directly in their course. Soon after, they came in sight of a low country, thickly wooded, which they called, in consequence, Markland. Probably this was Nova Scotia. After a few days they arrived at a place where they found the wild vines growing, and called it Vinland. Here they spent the winter. Some of the inhabitants of the country came to them in leather boats, and they traded with them for furs. The Norse legends call these people Skraelings. Probably they were Esquimaux (pronounced *Es-ki-mo*), as they are described as being of dwarfish stature and swarthy complexion. It is believed that Vinland was the northern part of Rhode Island, where the fox-grape still grows wild. Besides, the story mentions that, at that place, the sun remained nine hours above the horizon, on the shortest day. This would indicate the latitude of Rhode Island. The Norsemen returned to Greenland in the spring, and spread enthusiastic accounts of their new dwelling-place, praising the climate and soil, the grapes and salmon. The consequence was that large parties of the Northmen set sail for the new country and there founded a colony.

5. How long this settlement existed is not known; but at length it was abandoned, probably owing to the hostility of the Skraelings. The Norsemen sailed away from Vinland to return no more, and all traces of their colony disappeared. In course of time their colonies in Greenland were also abandoned. The memory of Helluland and Vinland almost faded away, and were only preserved in the Icelandic and Norwegian Sagas, or story-books, where they have been found in recent times. So far as is known, no European vessel followed in the track of the Northmen, or crossed the Atlantic in any other direction, for five hundred years, till

Columbus discovered the New World, far away to the south, at the close of the fifteenth century.

6. There can, however, be no doubt that these Northmen were the first white men who saw Newfoundland, and that they were familiar with portions of the northeast coast of America. It is also not improbable that traditions of their discoveries would linger among the people of Iceland for generations. Around their winter firesides, the old Icelanders would tell to English and Spanish sailors, who visited their shores, how their great-grandfathers had found a vine-growing country, far away to the west. Columbus is said to have made a voyage to Iceland, and these legends may have helped to fire his enthusiasm for discovery. Sailors from Bristol traded to Iceland, and may have carried the same tale to the ears of Cabot, who was to re-discover Newfoundland; and thus his hopes of finding land across the Atlantic, in the north-west, may have been strengthened.

7. At length the day arrived when these achievements of the pioneer Norsemen were to be altogether cast into the shade, and when the curtain that had so long shrouded the great continent of America from the eyes of Europeans was to be completely and for ever drawn aside. The fifteenth century was the age of geographical discoveries and maritime adventures. New ideas regarding the world and men's destiny in it began to make way. Suspicions arose in the minds of thoughtful men that the narrow strip of earth, consisting of parts of Europe, Asia, and Africa, — all that was then known, — could not be the whole. There was one man who had pondered deeply, for many years, on these secrets of the world. His name was Christopher Columbus, a native of Genoa in Italy. He was one of

the most skilful and fearless navigators of his day. In his mind at length arose the great thought, that by sailing out into those watery wastes which lay to the west, he would discover land. He by no means hoped to find a great continent, untrodden by the foot of any European; but he thought that by sailing westward, he

COLUMBUS.

would reach the eastern shores of Asia, and arrive at Cipango and Cathay, as Japan and China were then called. He fancied the globe to be much smaller than it is; and little suspected that a vast continent and the wide Pacific Ocean lay between him and Eastern Asia.

8. The great thought, dimly seen at first, rose grander and grander, and at length possessed the whole soul of Columbus. After great trials and difficulties,

and much opposition, he at length induced Ferdinand and Isabella, sovereigns of Spain, to intrust him with the command of three small ships, for purposes of discovery. The little squadron carried only one hundred and twenty men. On the 3d of August, 1492, he sailed from the port of Palos, in Andalusia; and on the 12th of October he landed on an island which he called San Salvador, one of the Bahamas. On that day connection between the two worlds began. A noble deed was done, such as can never be repeated — one that must stand alone in the records of time, encircling the name of the doer with imperishable renown. His discovery may be said to have doubled the habitable globe. Once and for ever the knowledge of a New World was secured for all men.

9. The daring achievement of Columbus was soon followed by another, which, though not so brilliant and dazzling, has secured for Cabot a fame second only to that of the discoverer of the New World. We can easily fancy what an effect on men's minds the news of Columbus's great discovery must have produced, as it flew from nation to nation. All the noble, energetic spirits of Europe longed to explore the wonders of the new country. Among those who felt this impulse most strongly were John Cabot and his son Sebastian, who were then living in the city of Bristol, a seaport on the west coast of England. John Cabot was a native of Venice, who had for some time resided in Bristol, where his children were born, and where he had successfully carried on business as a merchant. He was an intelligent, thoughtful man. His son Sebastian was an able navigator; and both father and son had given much attention to the great maritime enterprises which then filled the minds of men. To them the thought presented itself, that by taking a north-west course, instead of the track which had led Columbus to San Salvador, they would reach, by a shorter route, the eastern coasts of Asia. In this way they hoped to open up intercourse with the Cathay and Cipango, of which Marco Polo, the great traveller, had given such glowing accounts.

10. They had no trouble in inducing Henry VII., who then occupied the throne of England, to sanction their enterprise. This monarch was sorely mortified that he had not become the patron of Columbus, and thus shared in the honours and profits of his discoveries. He now readily listened to the bold project of the Cabots, and granted them "letters patent," authorizing their undertaking. With the parsimony for which he was noted, he left these men to bear all the expenses of the enterprise, and, in addition, bargained with them for a fifth part of all the profits. Not much credit is due to the king. The whole honour belongs to the Cabots, who adventured, not only their fortunes, but their lives, for the glory of their adopted country.

SEBASTIAN CABOT.

11. And so, early in the month of May, 1497, in a small caravel called "The Matthew," probably under one hundred tons burthen, these bold navigators sailed from the port of Bristol. Their course lay to the north-west, across the stormy wastes of the North Atlantic, where, since the days of the Northmen, European ship had never ventured.

12. Unfortunately, very few records of this voyage, from which such important consequences were to flow, have been preserved. But, in fancy, we can follow the little vessel, as it ploughs its way over the heaving billows of an unknown sea. We can see, in imagination, the resolute commander and his heroic son, as they pace the deck, vigilant, hopeful, breathing courage into the hearts of the half-terrified sailors, blessing every breeze that wafts them away from the habitations of civilized men. Onward the little vessel glides, a mere speck upon the waters. On the evening of June 23d the sun went down on the weary round of waters, and as yet there was no sign of land. Hope began to waver. But as the mist cleared away on the morning of June 24th, the glad cry of "Land Ho!" rang out from the masthead of "The Matthew," and a round of hearty cheers from stout English sailors greeted the first sight of the island of Newfoundland. We can fancy how glad and thankful these brave men must have felt at the successful termination of their perilous voyage.

13. For a long time it was doubtful what part of the New World was first seen by Cabot, and named by him "Prima Vista." Some said it was Cape Bonavista, on the eastern coast of Newfoundland. Others declared it was a part of the Labrador coast. Such doubts have lately been set at rest by the discovery of a map, bearing the date of 1544, and made by Sebastian Cabot, or under his direction. This map shows that his "Prima Vista" was near the eastern point of the present island of Cape Breton. After making land here, Cabot appears to have steered in a north-westerly direction, passing round Prince Edward Island; then north-easterly, till he fell in with the coast of Labrador; and then homeward, through the Straits of Belle Isle, round the north of Newfoundland.

AMERIGO VESPUCCI.

The main fact, however, is, that on this first voyage he discovered Newfoundland, and was also the discoverer of the continent of America. At this date, only some of the West India islands had been discovered by Columbus; and Amerigo Vespucci (pronounced Ah-$m\bar{a}$-re-go Ves-$poot$-$ch\bar{e}$), whose name has been given to the New World, had not made his first voyage across the Atlantic at the period of Cabot's discovery. Thus, the honour of discovering continental America belongs of right to Cabot.

14. As there is no mention of John Cabot after this time, it is probable that he did not long survive his first famous voyage. His son Sebastian now took his place as a discoverer. In the following year, 1498, he was authorized by King Henry to sail again, with six ships, to the land and islands which he had found. On this second expedition he sailed along the coast of Labrador to the 60th degree of north latitude. Deterred by the cold and ice from proceeding farther, he turned south, and coasted as far as the 38th degree, and then returned to England. Thus, by right of discovery, he secured for England a claim to Newfoundland and the neighbouring islands, and also to the whole coast of North America, from Hudson's Bay to Florida. He did for England as much as Columbus had done for Spain.

15. On his return from the first voyage, King Henry, with his characteristic stinginess, presented John Cabot with a gratuity of ten pounds. An entry of this shabby transaction has been found in the privy-purse accounts in the following words: "August 10th, 1497, To Hym that found the New Isle, £10." But the English people appreciated his worth and great services better than their king. They followed him in crowds, wherever he appeared, to pay him honour; called him "The Great Admiral"; and he could have enlisted as many of them as he pleased for his future voyages.

16. Sebastian Cabot made a third voyage, on which he is said to have sailed as far south as Cuba. For many years he lived in England, honoured and admired for his kind, modest disposition. He was ever urging on new maritime and commercial adventures. In company with others, he was the first to open up a trade between England and Russia. After a time he entered the service of the King of Spain, and was the discoverer of Brazil and the explorer of the Plata and Paraguay rivers. In the reign of Edward VI., he returned to England, and was appointed Chief Pilot of the kingdom, with a pension. He died in his eightieth year, in London. It is told of him that, on his dying bed, his thoughts often turned to the sea, whose mysterious secrets he had pondered for three-score years, and over whose billows his adventurous youth had opened a pathway. In the fevered wanderings of his mind he spoke of a new and infallible method of finding the longitude which had been divinely revealed to him, but which he was not permitted to disclose to any mortal.

17. It was said of him that "he gave England a continent — and no one knows his burial-place." It may be added that, in all that continent, there is not a spot called by his name, with the exception of one small island on the eastern coast of Newfoundland, to which was recently given the name of Cabot's Island.

QUESTIONS FOR EXAMINATION ON CHAPTER I.

1. Describe the situation of Newfoundland. Give the dimensions of the island. Why is its position so important?

2. Who were the Northmen? What were they noted for? Give an account of their colonies in Iceland and Greenland.

3. Describe the way in which the Northmen were led to discover America. What name did they give Newfoundland, and why?

4. Where were their Markland and Vinland? Who were their leaders on this expedition? What people did they meet with in Vinland?

5. Why did they abandon their colony in Vinland? Where was the story of their discoveries preserved?

6. How might it have been possible for Columbus and Cabot to hear of their voyages?

7. What was the fifteenth century noted for? Who was Columbus? What was the great thought which he cherished? Where did he hope to arrive by sailing west?

8. Who assisted him on his first voyage? Give the dates of his departure and arrival. Where did he land? What makes his discovery so great?

9. Give an account of John Cabot and his son Sebastian. What course did they propose to take, and what country did they hope to reach?

10. What did Henry VII. do to assist the Cabots?

11. When did Cabot sail? Name of the vessel?

12. Give an account of the voyage. What land was discovered, and on what day?

13. Where was Cabot's "Prima Vista"? What different opinions about it have been held? What was Cabot's course home? Who first discovered the continent of America?

14. Describe Cabot's second voyage. What were its results?

15. What reward did Henry VII. give Cabot? How did the English people regard him?

16. Give a sketch of the remaining portion of Cabot's life? Mention his further discoveries. How were his thoughts employed on his death-bed?

17. How was his memory neglected? Does any place bear his name?

MAP QUESTIONS.

Give the boundaries of Newfoundland. Where are the Straits of Belle Isle? Gulf of St. Lawrence? Labrador? Cape Breton? Show the positions of Norway, Iceland, Greenland, Rhode Island. Where are Genoa, Venice, Palos, San Salvador? Trace the course of Columbus to the Bahamas. Point out Japan and China. Where is Bristol? Trace Cabot's first voyage.

NOTES AND EXPLANATIONS IN CHAPTER I.

The Northmen. — In the ninth and tenth centuries, the Norsemen, or Vikings, were the terror of Christendom. From their rugged strongholds in Norway and Denmark, they issued in their light barques, ravaging the shores of Southern Europe, carrying terror and destruction wherever they went. Their skill in the management of their ships was marvellous. The affrighted dwellers on the shore saw them fearlessly careering over the stormiest seas, with all sails set. No port was safe from their attacks. Passing up the rivers in their small boats, they assailed the inland towns, burning and slaying. They were heathen of the most ferocious type, without fear or pity. They regarded the sea as their proper domain, and all that was to be found on it as their lawful prey. England felt the weight of their strong arms. They ravaged its cities and planted a powerful kingdom within its boundaries, which required all the skill and courage of the Saxon King Alfred to subdue. In France the Northmen seized and held Normandy, and from this vantage ground, in 1066, they invaded and conquered Saxon England. With all their wild energy and destructiveness, we can now see, on calmly looking back, that this people, mingling with the other nations of Europe, imparted to them many elements of valor, strength, and greatness. The English of to-day have a large mixture of Scandinavian blood in their veins, to which they owe some of their best qualities. Such were the wild sea-rovers who, before all other pale-faced men, looked on the shores of Newfoundland, and first colonized the American continent.

The Norsemen's Sagas. — Saga is a Norse word, and denotes a tale or poem founded on oral tradition, and gradually moulded into a written form. The old Icelandic, Norwegian, and Danish literature has of late years engaged the attention of scholars, and consists largely of these half-historical, half-mythical sagas, some of which have been translated into English. They belong from the ninth to the thirteenth centuries. The Royal Society of Northern Antiquarians at Copenhagen has given special attention to this literature.

Christopher Columbus. — Born at Genoa about the year 1435. He was the son of a cloth-weaver. When a youth, he acquired a good knowledge of the Latin language, and of geometry, astronomy, and navigation. At the age of fourteen he went to sea, being drawn to it by an irresistible longing. For twenty years he was either constantly voyaging or making charts. When thirty-five years of age he came to Portugal, drawn by the fame of its sea-captains and maritime discoveries. Thence he passed to Spain, and obtained the patronage of Ferdinand and Isabella. When he returned after his great discovery, he was received with all the honors of a triumphant conqueror; and the poor Genoese sailor became the most famous man in all the world. He made three more voyages, in the last of which he discovered, in 1498, the mainland of America, at the mouth of the river Orinoco. Yet he never knew that he had discovered a new continent, and died in the belief that what he had found was the eastern coast of Asia. He soon found the worthlessness of popularity. Seven years after his discovery he was sent home a prisoner in chains from the land he had found. On his return from his final expedition, broken in health and spirits, his noble patroness, Queen Isabella, was dead, and the ungrateful Ferdinand received him coldly, refused to restore him his offices and property, of which he had been unjustly deprived, and left him to spend his last days in poverty and neglect. He died on the 20th of May, 1506, at the age of seventy. His remains were interred first in Valladolid; afterwards carried to Seville; then taken across the Atlantic to St. Domingo; and finally, two hundred and fifty years afterwards to Havana, in the island of Cuba. In the Cathedral of Havana, on the right hand of the high altar, is an insignificant mural tablet, with a Latin inscription. There is nothing else to mark the grave of the Discoverer of the New World. But he whose monument is a whole continent needs no inscription on marble to perpetuate his deeds, which are indelibly inscribed on the memory of mankind.

Sebastian Cabot. — The memory of Cabot has received a similar unworthy treatment. His maps, charts, and journals, documents of immense value, were never published, and were either lost through carelessness or wilfully destroyed. Nicholls, in his Memoir of Cabot, who was one of the noblest and bravest men who ever trod an English deck, says, "The date of his death, like that of his birth, is unknown, and we can only infer that it was in or near London, from the fact that Richard Eden, his faithful and attached friend, who lived there, was present. Even where his ashes lie is a mystery; and he who gave to England a continent, and to Spain an empire, lies in some unknown tomb. This man, who surveyed and depicted three thousand miles of a coast which he had discovered; who gave to Britain, not only the continent, but the untold riches of the deep, in the fisheries of Newfoundland, and the whale fishery of the Arctic Sea; who, by his uprightness and fair dealing, raised England's name high among the nations, placed her credit on a solid foundation and made her citizens respected; who was the father of free trade, and gave us the carrying trade of the world; this man has not a statue in the city that gave him birth, or in the metropolis of the country he so greatly enriched, or a name on the land he discovered. Emphatically the most scientific seaman of his own, or, perhaps, many subsequent ages, — one of the gentlest, bravest, best of men, — his actions have been misrepresented, his discoveries denied, his deeds ascribed to others, and calumny has flung its filth on his memory."

The world knows not its prophets; stones them when living, leaving after ages to build their sepulchres.

Amerigo Vespucci, — or Americus Vespucius, as he is commonly called, — was born in Florence at 1451. Under the auspices of the King of Portugal, he made two voyages to South America, of which he published accounts, declaring himself the discoverer of the mainland of the Western Continent. Some years afterwards a German geographer proposed that the name America should be given to the new land, in his honour. By some strange caprice of fortune the proposal found acceptance, and Columbus's claims to name the land he had discovered were unjustly set aside.

Marco Polo.— Born at Venice. He visited in 1272 the court of Kublai Khan, the ruler of Chinese Tartary, who intrusted him with missions to China and India. He was the first European who visited China proper. After his many wanderings, he returned home and wrote an account of his travels, which excited the greatest interest, and helped to kindle the passion for discovery in the lands he had traversed in the mind of Columbus himself.

"Prima Vista." — Though Cabot's map seemed to indicate the eastern point of Cape Breton Island as the first land he approached, — or his "Prima Vista," — yet as Newfoundland is but fifty or sixty miles distant from that point, and was probably seen soon after as the vessel glided along the coast, and as most of the histories of the voyage represent Newfoundland as the first land discovered by Cabot, I have followed the common account in the text, and represented the sailors of "The Matthew" as greeting the sight of the island with British cheers.

CHRONOLOGICAL SUMMARY. — MEMORABLE EVENTS AND PERSONS OF THE PERIOD.

A. D.
- 1001. Newfoundland and the Continent of America discovered by the Northmen.
- 1015. Canute the Great (Dane) on the throne of England.
- 1042. Edward the Confessor.
- 1066. William the Conqueror.
- 1096. First Crusade, led by Peter the Hermit.
- 1147. Second Crusade, led by Louis VII. of France.
- 1189. Richard I. of England began to reign.
  Third Crusade, led by Frederic Barbarossa, Philip Augustus, and Richard of England.
- 1215. Magna Charta obtained.
- 1270. Eighth and last Crusade.
- 1311. Suppression of the Knights Templar.
- 1343. Cannon first used.
- 1346. Battle of Crécy.
  Distinguished authors of the fourteenth century — Dante, Petrarch, Boccaccio, Chaucer, Froissart.
- 1431. Joan of Arc burned.
- 1435. Christopher Columbus born.
- 1452. Invention of printing.
- 1455. Wars of the Roses begun.
- 1472. Sebastian Cabot born at Bristol.
- 1474. First book printed in England.
- 1479. Union of the Kingdom of Ferdinand and Isabella.
- 1485. Henry VII. of England began to reign.
- 1492. America discovered by Columbus.
- 1497. Newfoundland and the Continent of America discovered by the Cabots.
- 1498. Coast of America explored by Sebastion Cabot.
  Continent of America discovered by Columbus.
- 1499. Amerigo Vespucci visited South America.
- 1506. Death of Columbus.

CHAPTER II.

THE RED INDIANS, OR ABORIGINAL INHABITANTS OF NEWFOUNDLAND.

THEIR ORIGIN. — MEMBERS OF THE ALGONQUIN FAMILY. — THEIR MODES OF LIFE. — SAD FATE.

1. When the island of Newfoundland was discovered by Cabot it was found to be inhabited by a savage tribe of Red Indians, who lived by hunting and fishing. They called themselves Bethucks or Bœothics. Their appearance and modes of life prove that they were a branch of the race of red men who were found spread over the whole continent of North America. At what time this tribe wandered away from the parent stock, and found their way to Newfoundland, is utterly unknown. Most likely they crossed originally from Canada, by the Straits of Belle Isle, or from the neighbouring island of Cape Breton.

However this may have been, they were widely spread over the island when the white men arrived. In all probability, for many centuries before, they had been hunting the reindeer and bear, trapping the otter, fox, and beaver, and gliding over the lakes and rivers in their birch canoes. The herds of reindeer, the ptarmigan, wild geese and ducks, the salmon, codfish, and seals, must have given them food in abundance. The skins of the animals they slaughtered, and the rich furs which were the spoils of the chase, supplied them with clothing. They had a method of preparing these skins for use by smoking them, instead of tanning, as is now the practice.

For this wild, roving people it was an evil day when the pale-faces appeared. Then began those conflicts, cruelties, and miseries which at length ended in the complete extinction of the race. In the whole of the island not a single representative of this once numerous tribe now exists. Only a few relics, consisting of their arrow-heads, hatchets, and other stone implements, have been preserved. Some of these, and also a single skull of one of the race, are now in the Geological Museum in St. John's, and they are nearly all the traces of the Red Indians now left.

2. When Europeans began to explore the continent of America, north and south, they found it occupied by a people very unlike themselves. They named them "Indians," because they supposed the country to be only the eastern part of Asia, or India, as it was then generally called. Finding their mistake afterwards, they called this strange people "American Indians." They presented a great diversity in appearance and modes of life; and yet there was a family likeness, common to them all, which has led learned men to conclude that they were all descended from the same stock. Their origin is unknown. They were all of the same swarthy and copper colour; had long, straight, black hair, high cheek-bones, long eyes, and scanty beards. The most natural division of them is into two great families, one called the Toltecan, and the other the American. The Toltecan nations include the Mexicans, Peruvians, and Chilians, who were found in a much more advanced state of civilization than the American division, which comprehended all the barbarous tribes of the New World.

3. It is believed that the whole of the American aborigines numbered in the vicinity of 20,000,000 when the Europeans arrived. Those tribes who lived along

the Atlantic coast of North America occupied both sides of the Alleghany mountains, from the Gulf of Mexico to Canada and New Brunswick. Nearly all of these belonged to two great families, called the Algonquins and the Iroquois. The Algonquins were spread over the space between the river Mississippi and the Atlantic, and as far north as Hudson's Bay. They all spoke dialects of the same language. This great family included such tribes as the Ottawas, Ojibways, Chippewas, Abenaquis, and many more. The Iroquois, called also the "Five Nations" and the "Six Nations," lived to the south of the great lakes of Canada, and comprehended such tribes as the Mohawks, Hurons, Senecas, and many besides. They also spoke dialects of one language. It is believed that both together numbered a quarter of a million of Indians.

4. The question arises, to which of the two great families did the Indians of Newfoundland belong? From an examination of their language learned men are satisfied that they were a branch of the wide-spread and warlike Algonquins. In their habits, appearance, and mode of life they resembled the Algonquin tribes who lived in Nova Scotia, Cape Breton, and Canada.

5. Cabot said of them: "The inhabitants of this island use the skins and furs of wild beasts for garments, which they hold in as high estimation as we do our finest clothes. In war they use bows and arrows, spears, darts, clubs, and slings." Like the other Indians they shaved their hair, except one lock, called the "scalplock," which was tied on the top, and ornamented with birds' feathers. The women wore their hair long, and had closer-fitting garments than the men, and their waists girded. They had an original method of kindling fire, by striking together two pieces of iron pyrites,—a

kind of stone which is very common in the island. Their bows were of sycamore or mountain ash, the strings being of deer's sinews. Their arrows were of well-seasoned pine, light, and perfectly straight, the heads being of stone sharpened to a fine point. They were able to make fish-hooks of bone, and nets out of vegetable fibres.

6. They lived in wigwams, the frames of which were made of poles, and covered with birch-bark, or skins, through which was an opening for the smoke to escape. Some of these winter wigwams were large enough to contain eighteen or twenty people; and a dozen or more of them, when placed together, formed an Indian village. It has been found, on examining the remains of some of these wigwams, that around the fireplaces they dug small hollows in the ground, like nests, and lined them with dry moss, or the soft branches of trees. In these they sat, and probably slept. The soft, warm lining must have added greatly to their comfort in the cold nights of winter. They were able to make vessels out of the rind of spruce trees, sufficiently strong to stand the heat of boiling water, and in these they cooked their meat.

7. Perhaps the most wonderful of all their contrivances were their deer-fences. In order to capture the deer, during their annual migrations from north to south, they constructed fences along the banks of rivers, such as the Exploits. These were sometimes thirty or forty miles in length. The labour of erecting them and keeping them in repair was very great, and shows that they must have been a numerous tribe to accomplish so much work. Openings were left in these fences, at different places, for the deer to go through and swim across the rivers. At these spots the Indians were

stationed, and with their spears slaughtered the deer when in the water, out of their canoes. The fences were made by felling trees along the banks, without chopping their trunks quite through, and taking care that each tree, as it fell, took the proper direction, and joined on to the last which had been cut. Any gaps were filled by driving in stakes and interweaving branches of trees. They were from eight to ten feet high, so that no deer could overleap them.

8. Their canoes were made of the bark of the white birch, were light, often gracefully shaped, and could be easily paddled, as they drew little water. The whole rind of a birch tree was stripped off, without being torn, and then put round a light frame. The edges were sewed together with thongs, made of the tough roots of certain trees, and the seams were covered with a kind of pitch, made from the gum of trees, so as to render them water-tight. When injured the canoe could be easily patched with pieces of bark, fastened in the same way.

9. The Indian snow-shoe was made by stretching a net-work of deer's hide on a light frame, three or four feet long, curved and tapering. The net-work was fastened to the foot by thongs, and the foot was covered only with a light moccason, made of deer-skin. On these shoes an Indian could travel forty miles a day, and even run down a deer whose hoofs cut through the crust of the snow.

10. The Indians of Newfoundland, like those of the continent, were tall, well-proportioned, robust, but not equal to Europeans in bodily strength. They had not such strong arms, and could not strike such heavy blows. But they were active, light of foot, and possessed wonderful powers of endurance. Their carriage was graceful and dignified. So keen were their perceptions that

they could make their way through a trackless forest with ease simply by observing the appearance of the moss and bark upon the trees. They had the virtues and vices of savage life. They were devoted to their tribe; faithful to one another; brave, and possessed of a wonderful fortitude; but in war they were fierce, vindictive, merciless, and cruel to prisoners. They treated their women with cruelty, and made them work like beasts of burden. They had no idea of restraining their animal appetites, and ate voraciously when food was plentiful, without any regard to the future.

11. The early voyagers to the shores of the island described them as lively, tractable, and disposed to be friendly with white men. The good understanding, unhappily, did not last long. When the settlers began to spread over the shores of the island they seized on the best fishing-stations, and drove away the Indians. Quarrels arose. Doubtless there were faults on both sides. The savages, when opportunity offered, stole the goods of the whites. To them such objects as knives, hatchets, nails, and lines, presented a temptation almost irresistible. The rude fishermen and trappers of those days were an immoral, lawless order of men, and punished the thefts of the savages mercilessly. These, again, retaliated fiercely; and thus a state of savage warfare was established, and terrible deeds were done. The red man became the implacable foe of the white man; and the latter regarded the Indians as vermin, to be hunted down and destroyed. That the poor savages were treated with brutal cruelty admits of no doubt.

12. But what could clubs and arrows avail against fire-arms? Gradually the red men were reduced in numbers. They were driven from their fishing-posts on the bays and rivers; their hunting-grounds were invaded by

the furriers. Hunger and disease thinned their ranks. Another tribe of Indians, from Nova Scotia, called Micmacs, attacked them, and had the advantage of knowing the use of fire-arms. Slowly, but surely, the unhappy tribe wasted away, and at length disappeared from the face of the earth.

13. Before they were quite exterminated the spirit of humanity awoke, and zealous efforts were made to save them from destruction. Proclamations forbidding any one to injure them, under heavy penalties, were issued by the British government. An expedition was sent to the river Exploits. to open friendly communica-

WIGWAM POINT, RIVER EXPLOITS.

tions with them, but ended disastrously. A female called Mary March. from the month in which she was captured by some hunters on Red Indian Lake, was brought to St. John's. in 1819. She was treated with great kindness, and sent back to her tribe with presents, but died on the way. Another Indian woman, called in her language Shanandithet, was also taken at a later date. She lived six years in St. John's, and died of consumption. She declared she dared not go back to her tribe after having held intercourse with the whites, as they would kill her. When, in 1828, an exploring party was sent by some benevolent persons to their head-quarters at Red Indian Lake, not a living Bœothic could be found. Thus the efforts to atone for past wrongs and cruelties were too late, and proved fruitless.

QUESTIONS FOR EXAMINATION ON CHAPTER II.

1. Who were the inhabitants of Newfoundland at the time of its discovery? By what name were they known? To what family of the American Indians did they belong? How did they live? What effect had the arrival of Europeans on their destiny? What relics of them are in existence?

2. Why were the aboriginal inhabitants of America called Indians? Describe their appearance. Into what two families have they been divided? Who were Toltecans?

3. What was the number of the aborigines of America when Columbus arrived? What two great families of Indians occupied the Atlantic coast of North America? Where did each of them live?

4. To which of them did the Indians of Newfoundland belong? What proofs are given?

5. What did Cabot say of the Newfoundland Indians? How did they wear their hair? How did they kindle fire? Describe their bows, arrows, fish-hooks.

6. Describe their wigwams. What contrivance had they for warmth around their fireplaces?

7. Describe their deer-fences. How were they made? What was their height?

8. How were their canoes made? How repaired?

9. Describe their snow-shoes. How far could they travel in a day?

10. What was their personal appearance? How did they make their way through a forest? What were their virtues and vices? How did they treat their women?

11. How did the white settlers treat the Indians? What were the causes of quarrels?

12. How were they reduced in numbers? What Indian tribe attacked them?

13. What efforts were made to save the Indians from destruction? Who were Mary March and Shanandithet? When was the last effort made to find them, and what its result?

MAP QUESTIONS.

Point out the region of North America occupied by Algonquin and Iroquois Indians. Where is Red Indian Lake? What river flows through it? Trace the Exploits from its head-waters to its outlet.

NOTES AND EXPLANATIONS. — CHAPTER II.

The Religion of the Indians. — Little is known of the religious ideas and observances of the red men of Newfoundland. Like the other tribes of North America, they probably believed in the existence of a Supreme Being, whom they called the Great Spirit; and also of an inferior spirit, whose nature was malicious and evil. Their worship was chiefly addressed to the evil spirit with a view of propitiating him. They thought the Good Spirit needed no prayers to secure his protection and blessing. Their religious observances consisted chiefly of songs and dances, with much noise and excitement. They believed that all animals had protecting spirits, and that the winds and the stars had also spirits. In Longfellow's poem of "Hiawatha" many of their legends and religious ideas and ceremonies have been preserved. In some of their graves around Red Indian Lake have been found bows, arrows, and other weapons, and articles of property which had belonged to the deceased in their lifetime. This indicated that the Bethucks believed they would live again after death, and use these weapons in the happy hunting-grounds of the blest in heaven. All brave warriors and good women were to be happy there forever, following the same pursuits as on earth.

Numbers of the Indians. — Within the limits of the United States there are now about 150,000 Indians, who are cared for by the government. Only a few of them have adopted habits of civilized life. Altogether there are 500,000 Indians, in the United States. In the older provinces of Canada there are 30,000 Indians who are in charge of a department of the State. Including British Columbia, the North-west, and Labrador, the Indians and Esquimaux in the whole of the Dominion of Canada number 132,000. In both countries they are diminishing in numbers, and in fifty or a hundred years few will probably remain.

Haunts of the Indians. — They appear to have inhabited chiefly the north-eastern, northern, and north-western portions of Newfoundland. Many of their implements and weapons have been dug up on the shores of Trinity and Bonavista Bays, at Fogo and Twillingate, and in White Bay. Their head-quarters were in the neighbourhood of Red

Indian Lake. When Cormack, the traveller who crossed Newfoundland in 1822, penetrated to Red Indian Lake, in 1828, he found numerous ruins of their winter and summer wigwams, their storehouses for smoking and drying venison; also, a large canoe, twenty-two feet in length. He could find no living Indian. In a wooden hut, well protected from wild animals and the weather, he found the bodies of two grown persons laid out on the floor, wrapped in deer-skins. This was one of their modes of burial. In the same place was the body of Mary March, in a white coffin. When she died her remains were left in this coffin, at the seaside, and had been conveyed by the members of her tribe to this burying-place. With Cormack's expedition the last hope of finding any of the Red Indians was abandoned. No trace of them has been discovered since his day.

Their Intellectual Faculties.—The Bethucks did not advance beyond the savage state. They were not, however, inferior to the Canadian tribes. The whole race of American Indians were greatly inferior to Europeans, and even to Mongolians, in mental powers. In constructive and imitative faculties they were very low; and to this day, though in contact with white men, they have made little progress.

CHAPTER III.

FROM 1497 TO 1534.

EXPLORATION AND SETTLEMENT OF AMERICA.

THE SPANISH, FRENCH, AND ENGLISH. — IMPORTANCE OF THE NEWFOUNDLAND FISHERIES.

1. Now that the New World was discovered, and some idea obtained of its vast extent, the question arose, who were to explore it and take possession of it? The most wonderful tales were told about it. Sailors, and other adventurers who had been there, related stories about rivers which flowed over pebbles of gold, and sands sparkling with precious gems; of vast forests, and lovely flowers, in lands teeming with fertility. Here was a boundless field for human energy. The wildest hopes of obtaining vast wealth were kindled; and all the adventurous spirits of Europe were eager to undertake voyages to the new land. The Spaniards, who were the first discoverers, rushed away in such multitudes upon these expeditions that some large towns in Spain lost half their inhabitants. Portugal and France followed in the same track, and England was not far behind. Immediate gain was the object of every one. Gold was the grand attraction.

2. All the great nations of Europe thought they had a right to seize and hold whatever portion of the new continent they had discovered or explored. But at first they had no great desire to stay there and keep possession. They wanted to plunder, or find gold and silver to enrich themselves, then to return to their own country

and enjoy their wealth. Only a few thought of trading with these new countries. They did not wish to settle and make homes for themselves across the Atlantic. Nearly a hundred years elapsed, after Columbus's discovery, before the great idea of colonizing America took firm hold of the European mind.

3. The Spaniards early obtained possession of the West India Islands. The conquest of Mexico by Cortes, in 1521, and of Peru by Pizarro, speedily followed. The immense plunder obtained in these countries failed to satiate their thirst for gold, and the Spaniards began to look towards North America. There was at that time an aged Spanish warrior, named Ponce de Leon, who, in his youth, had distinguished himself in fighting against the Moors in Spain. He had been a companion of Columbus, on his second voyage, and was afterwards appointed Governor of Porto Rico; but, being displaced, he returned to Spain. Among the strange tales which were told in these credulous times was one about a " Fountain of Youth," which was said to exist in this new land. It was believed to have the power of restoring youth, with all its powers, to the happy man who bathed in its ever-flowing waters. He who was fortunate enough to find it obtained the secret of perpetual youth. Ponce de Leon was an old man, and he resolved to find this wonderful fountain. He wanted also to renew his fortune, as well as his youth, by the riches he hoped to find. And so, in 1512, he sailed westward from Porto Rico; and on Easter Sunday, which the Spaniards called Pascua Florida, or Flowery Easter, he came in sight of a new land, to which he gave the name of Florida. The country was then beautiful with the opening blossoms of spring, so that the name seemed appropriate in a double sense. Ponce de

Leon did not find in the flowery land the "Fountain of Youth," but something very different, when, on a second visit, five years later, he received his death-wound from an Indian arrow. But he found for Spain a new province, and a new channel for commerce through the Gulf of Florida. Fifty years afterwards, near the spot where he first landed, the town of St. Augustine was founded, and it is the oldest in the United States.

4. Great results followed this search for the "Fountain of Youth." Fabulous stories were told about Florida, and it was reported to be the richest country in the world, abounding in gold and gems. Another Spanish noble, named De Soto, heard and believed these tales, and determined to possess himself of the riches of Florida. He organized an expedition composed of 600 men, splendidly armed and equipped, among whom were the very flower of Spanish youth, full of hope and courage, and eager for discovering new lands and plundering their inhabitants. He landed on Florida in 1539, and, with his men, began the march northward into the interior. The Indians were hostile and fought against the invaders. No gold was found; scarcely could food be obtained. Terrible hardships were endured. No rich cities, like those in Mexico and Peru, were found, but only poor villages of savage tribes. Sickness thinned their ranks. At length De Soto, to his astonishment, arrived at the banks of a magnificent river, a mile in width, having a current of great strength. In the Old World there was nothing to be compared to this majestic stream. It was the Mississippi, the "Father of Waters," now first seen by Europeans. The Spaniards managed to cross it, and for many months wandered among the dreary swamps and gloomy forests of this region. At length, broken in health and spirit, De

Soto died. His men formed a rude coffin out of the trunk of a pine tree, and, in the darkness of the night, sunk his body in the middle of the river, that his death should not be known to the Indians, who might treat his remains with indignity. He rested beneath the waters of the river he had discovered. His men constructed some rude vessels, and floated down the Mississippi to the Gulf of Mexico. Only 300 managed to escape, and they reached Cuba in a wretched plight.

5. Important consequences were to follow from these disastrous failures of the first explorers. On the strength of this discovery of Florida, Spain, at one time, claimed as her own the whole coast of North America as far as, and including, Newfoundland; and even to the extreme north of the continent. The name North America was not then heard of, and Spain called the whole Florida, and claimed it as part of her vast dominions. Yet she had not occupied a harbour, or marked out a settlement, or built a fortification, on the whole coast, and had acquired no right by discovery, excepting over Florida.

6. These vast claims, on the part of Spain, were not at first disputed by any other power. France, however, was now about to enter the field, and to contend for her share of the New World. Gradually, as events disclosed themselves, and discoveries extended, a grand scheme was formed, in the minds of French monarchs and statesmen, of creating a " New France," with feudal institutions, in the western hemisphere. This plan was pursued by the French with determined energy for two centuries and a half. It was in carrying this scheme of empire into execution that they were brought to Newfoundland, and tried so often to conquer and annex it. Indeed, at one time, it seemed as if France was to be the ruling power in North America.

7. The attention of France was first drawn to North America by the discovery of the fisheries of Newfoundland. The same holds good regarding England. The attraction which first led Englishmen to these western seas, and awoke in the national mind an impulse to colonize these new countries, was the immense fish wealth in the seas around the island discovered by Cabot. Here, they saw, was an inexhaustible supply of the finest food, at a time when fish, salted and fresh, entered very largely into the diet of the people. France and England early engaged in the prosecution of the cod-fisheries on the Banks and around the shores of Newfoundland. Both nations drew enormous wealth, year after year, from these industries, and thus increased their national greatness. The English and French fishermen engaged in these fisheries supplied the navy and mercantile marine of both nations with bold and skilful sailors, and thus developed their power at sea. Both nations found here the best nurseries for seamen. Both were thus drawn to the region of the St. Lawrence, and were led to plant colonies, originally with a view to carry on the fisheries. The rivalry between the two powers for obtaining the sovereignty of the soil arose in connection with the fisheries. The long wars between France and England were avowedly for the fisheries and the territories around them. Thus the fisheries of Newfoundland really laid the foundation of the empire which England at length acquired in America, when her supremacy was established, after a long contest with France. These fisheries were far more influential in bringing about the settlement of North America than all the gold of Mexico and Peru accomplished in Southern America.

8. The humble, industrious fishermen, who plied their hard labours along the shores and on the Banks of Newfoundland, and in the neighbouring seas, were the pioneers of the great host from the Old World who, in due time, built up the United States and overspread Canada. They have done an honourable stroke of work in the great business of the world. England owes much to them. Till these fisheries drew her seamen from their narrow seas, and taught them to brave the storms of the Atlantic, her merchant marine was of small account, and her navy had scarcely an existence. In prosecuting these fisheries England learned how to become mistress of the seas. It was in Newfoundland, too, that the great mother of colonies made her first attempt at colonization. Here her flag first waved over her possessions in the western hemisphere. Newfoundland is her oldest colony.

QUESTIONS FOR EXAMINATION ON CHAPTER III.

1. What wild tales were told about the New World? What effect had these stories? What nations engaged in exploring it?

2. What was supposed to give a right of possession? What was the chief object of adventurers?

3. Who were Cortes and Pizarro? Who was Ponce de Leon? What did he go in search of? Why was Florida so called? What was the fate of Ponce de Leon?

4. Who was De Soto? Why did he visit Florida? How many men had he? Describe his march. What great river did he discover? Where was he buried?

5. Why did Spain claim all North America? Why were her claims unjust?

6. What scheme of empire did the French form?

7. What first drew the attention of the French and English to North America? Why were the fisheries so valuable to both nations? How did their navies and commerce profit by the Newfoundland fisheries? Why did the two nations go to war? How did English settlements begin?

8. Who were the pioneers in settling North America? Show the importance of these fisheries to England.

MAP QUESTIONS.

Where are Mexico, Peru, Porto Rico, Florida? Trace the course of the Mississippi. Point out its principal tributaries. Where are the Banks of Newfoundland?

NOTES AND EXPLANATIONS.—CHAPTER III.

Cortes.—Hernan Cortes was born in 1485, at a village of Estremadura in Spain. He distinguished himself in the conquest of Cuba, and was selected to undertake the conquest of Mexico. He sailed in 1518, with 10 vessels, 600 infantry, and 18 horsemen. After three years of desperate fighting and a terrible slaughter of the Mexicans he seized their emperor, Montezuma, took their capital, obtained immense quantities of gold, and completely conquered the kingdom. He returned to Spain, and died at Seville, in 1547.

Pizarro.—Francisco Pizarro, conqueror of Peru, was born in Estremadura, in 1476. He was with Balboa when he discovered the Pacific Ocean. In his various expeditions and voyages about Panama he discovered the vast and prosperous Peruvian empire, abounding in gold, silver, and precious stones. In 1529 he obtained from Charles V., of Spain, authority to conquer Peru. In 1531 he set out with 3 vessels, 180 men, and 27 horsemen. He was guilty of the direst cruelties and treacheries; but with a handful of men he defeated the hosts of Peruvians, took their capital, and executed their emperor. He lived at Lima almost like a king, but died by the hands of an assassin in 1541.

Florida.—Though Ponce de Leon gave Florida its name, Sebastian Cabot was its first discoverer, on his second voyage. It is now one of the United States, with a population of 200,000. It produces cotton, sugar, oranges, rice, tobacco. Owing to its fine climate it is now a resort of invalids. In 1763 Spain ceded Florida to England in exchange for Havana. It was reconquered by the Spaniards in 1781. In 1821 it was ceded by Spain to the United States.

The Mississippi.—One of the largest rivers on the globe. From Little Winnipeg Lake, its principal source, to its termination in the Gulf of Mexico, it is 3,200 miles in length. It drains an area of 1,210,000 square miles, or nearly one-seventh of North America. The valley through which it flows is called "the garden of the world," from its fertility. It receives the Missouri, Ohio, Illinois, Wisconsin rivers, and many others, and rolls its vast volume through eighteen degrees of latitude. Its discharge of water at its mouth is at the rate of 675,000 cubic feet per second.

CHAPTER IV.

FROM 1534 TO 1583.

ENGLAND TAKES POSSESSION OF NEWFOUNDLAND.

BRETON AND BASQUE FISHERMEN. — PROGRESS OF THE FRENCH IN CANADA. — ARRIVAL OF SIR HUMPHREY GILBERT.

1. Soon after Cabot spread the news of the abundance of fish of the finest quality, and in great variety, in Newfoundland waters, the French fishermen of Brittany and Normandy were engaged there in taking cod. They were the first to profit by this new discovery of Englishmen. These bold mariners ventured out into these stormy seas in their little cockle-shells of vessels, such as no one would now dream of using in crossing the Atlantic. They reached the Island of Cape Breton, and gave it the name it now bears, after their home in Bretagne, or Brittany. Seven years after Cabot's discovery, in 1504, these hardy fishermen were here, carrying on a profitable industry. They were soon followed by the fishermen of the Basque provinces, in the northwest of Spain, who were scarcely less daring at sea. They have left a memorial of their visits in the name of Port-aux-Basques, a fine harbour near Cape Ray, on the southern shore of Newfoundland. The Portuguese fishermen speedily took part in the same fisheries. A Portuguese navigator, named Gaspard Cortereal, had, in 1500, visited Newfoundland, and discovered and named Conception Bay and Portugal Cove, on its southern shore. The number of vessels and men engaged in

these fisheries rapidly increased. In 1517 40 sail of Portuguese, French, and Spaniards were thus employed. In 1527 John Rut, an English captain, visited St. John's, and wrote a letter, when there, to Henry VIII., in which he said he found in the harbour 11 sail of Normans, 1 Breton, and 2 Portuguese barques, but no English fishing-vessels. So late as 1578 there were 400 fishing-vessels employed, of which 150 were French, and only 50 were English, — so slow were they in following the lead of the other nations. England had not yet discovered the immense value of these fisheries, though increasing numbers of her fishermen were taking a part in them. Other nations were freely using the shores and harbours of the island discovered by Cabot; but as yet Englishmen made small account of it and its fisheries.

2. Meantime the wealth which France was deriving from these seas led her to form new and extensive designs of colonizing North America. Her claims to the possession of the northern part of the continent rested on the discoveries of John Verazzani (pronounced Ver-rat-tsah'-ne), a Florentine, who was employed by Francis I., King of France, to explore the new region. In 1524 he sailed from France, reached the coast of North Carolina, and then examined the whole coast to the northward. Passing the shores of what are now Virginia and Maryland, he entered the harbour of New York, which he found crowded with Indian canoes. Pursuing his voyage he coasted along Maine and Nova Scotia, and examined many miles of the shores of Newfoundland. He then returned to France, and wrote an account of his discoveries.

3. The career of discovery, thus opened, was eagerly pursued by France. Ten years later, in 1534, Jacques Cartier (Zhak Kar-te-ay), the famous Breton mariner

of St. Malo, sailed from that port with a commission from the French king. His voyage proved to be a momentous one in its consequences. He passed through

JACQUES CARTIER.

the Straits of Belle Isle, entered the Bay of Chaleur, unfurled the French flag at Gaspé, discovered the River St. Lawrence, and on his second voyage ascended it as far as Montreal, and built a fort at Quebec. Thus Cartier was the discoverer of Canada, and secured it for France. To a Frenchman belongs the honour of this great discovery; for the English never ascended the St. Lawrence in any of their early voyages. The hold thus obtained by France was not relinquished for two hundred and twenty-six years, when Quebec fell before the conquering arms of Wolfe.

4. Other adventurers followed in the track of Cartier. Roberval's expedition ended in disaster. De la Roche, fifty years after, was equally unfortunate. But the brave and high-minded Champlain and De Monts carried on the work of exploration, colonization, and the extension of French commerce, and thus laid the foundations of French empire in the West. All Canada and Acadia (the name given by the French to Nova Scotia and New Brunswick) was held by France. Newfoundland, with its fisheries, seemed likely to share the same fate. Marquette, a Jesuit Father, starting from the great lakes of Canada, followed the river Wisconsin till he reached the Mississippi, and sailed down the river for some distance. It was a deed of true heroism. La Salle, a French cavalier, followed courageously in the same course, and sailed down the Mississippi to its outlet in the Gulf of Mexico, — a memorable achievement. France then claimed all the vast territory through which the great river flowed; and La Salle named it Louisiana, in honour of Louis XIV.

5. Thus it looked as if there were to be no English settlements in North America. All the southern portion was called Florida, and belonged to Spain; and " New France" seemed destined to absorb all the rest. And yet the day was coming when neither France nor Spain would own a foot of land in the whole continent of America, north and south; and when, of all the vast possessions of France in the New World, her flag would wave over but two small islands, St. Pierre and Miquelon, at the mouth of Fortune Bay, Newfoundland.

6. All this time the English had never forgotten that Cabot and his stout west-country sailors had first discovered Newfoundland and the mainland of North America, which were theirs by right of discovery. And now, at length, the hour arrived for enforcing their rights, and claiming their share in the western world. The great movement was begun by taking formal possession of Newfoundland, and making a first, though unsuccessful, attempt to plant a colony there. This is the way in which it came about.

7. There was living in England, in the reign of Queen Elizabeth, a brave, patriotic nobleman, named Sir Humphrey Gilbert. His residence was Compton Castle, near

Torbay, in Devonshire. He had a half-brother, also a knight, called Sir Walter Raleigh, whose name is famous in English history. Sir Humphrey Gilbert had won high

SIR HUMPHREY GILBERT.

distinction as a soldier in his youth. In his mature manhood he gave much attention to navigation, geography, and the great discoveries which were then going on in the western hemisphere. He wrote a book, in which he tried to prove that it was possible to find a north-west passage to Eastern Asia. He had formed a very high opinion of the value of the Newfoundland fisheries. Many of the Devonshire fishermen were already engaged in these fisheries; and from some of the captains Sir Humphrey, no doubt, obtained his information. He considered that the right way to carry on these fisheries was by settling English people on the island, who could both fish and cultivate the soil, and make a home for themselves as well. Besides, he thought it a shame that his countrymen should be content to look on with indifference, while the French and Spaniards were dividing among themselves the soil and riches of the New World. He knew that England had acquired rights by discovery; and he believed that it was her duty to do her part in exploring and settling these new countries. and thus open a field for the enterprise of her people.

8. His half-brother. Sir Walter Raleigh, held the same views; and together they laid the matter before Queen Elizabeth. She at once gave Sir Humphrey letters-patent authorizing him to take possession of Newfoundland on her behalf. to colonize it. and to exercise jurisdiction over it and all the neighbouring lands within two hundred leagues in every direction.

SIR WALTER RALEIGH.

9. An expedition was organized. consisting of five vessels. Sir Walter Raleigh embarked in one of these; but an infectious disease broke out on board. and compelled him to return to port. Gilbert, with the other four vessels, reached the harbour of St. John's, early in August, 1583. The largest of these vessels, the "Delight." was only of 120 tons; the "Golden Hind," of 50 tons; the "Swallow." of 50 tons; and the "Squirrel. of 10 tons. The number of adventurers on board was 260, most of them Devonshire men.

10. At that time there were lying in the harbour of St. John's thirty-six vessels, of which nearly half were English; the rest were Portuguese, French, and Spanish, all engaged in fishing. On the 5th of August, 1583, Sir Humphrey, his officers and men, all landed. The captains and crews of the fishing-vessels were summoned to attend. In the midst of the motley assemblage the English knight stood up and read the patent authorizing him to take possession of the island on behalf of his royal mistress. After the custom of the times, twig and sod from the island were presented to him, and he solemnly declared Newfoundland a portion of the British empire. The banner of England was hoisted on a flagstaff; the royal arms, cut in lead, were affixed to a wooden pillar, near the water's edge; and with some rounds of hearty British cheers the ceremonial of the day was brought to a close.

11. Very soon, however, troubles arose. Many of the men on board Sir Humphrey's little fleet were not of the right stamp for colonists, and they became discontented and troublesome. Sickness broke out, and Gilbert sent the sick home in the "Swallow." With the remaining three vessels he set out, on the 20th August, to prosecute further explorations. He got as far as Cape Race, where his largest vessel, the "Delight," struck on a shoal and went to pieces. The brave captain, Morris Browne, refused to leave his ship, and perished with the greater part of those on board. Only 15 escaped in a boat, and reached land after terrible sufferings. Sir Humphrey had been on board the little "Squirrel," surveying the different harbours. Disheartened by the loss of his largest vessel, on board of which were most of the stores, he deemed it wise to return to England, especially as winter was at hand.

12. His men pressed him to go on board the "Golden Hind," the larger vessel; but the gallant knight said "he would not abandon his brave comrades whose perils he had shared," and he remained on board the little nutshell of a vessel, where his flag was flying. A terrible storm overtook them near the Azores. The "Golden Hind" kept as near the little "Squirrel" as possible, for every moment it seemed as if she would be swallowed up. In the midst of the tempest the crew of the larger ship saw the brave knight, who was a stranger to fear, sitting calmly on the deck, with a book before him, and heard him cry to his companions, "Cheer up, lads! We are as near heaven on sea as on land." The darkness of night closed in. Suddenly, about midnight, the lights of the "Squirrel" disappeared, and Sir Humphrey Gilbert and his men sank amid the dark billows of the Atlantic.

13. Thus perished one of the noblest and bravest of those who, in that age, sought to extend the dominion of England in the New World. The "Golden Hind" reached Falmouth a mere wreck. The first attempt to colonize Newfoundland ended thus disastrously, as, indeed, did most of the first efforts at planting colonies in the western hemisphere. The loss to Newfoundland of Sir Humphrey Gilbert was great and irreparable. Had he lived, and succeeded in planting a colony, then the cultivation of the soil would have gone on, hand in hand with the fisheries, and the wealth derived from the fisheries would have remained in the country for its improvement. A prosperous resident population would thus have grown up. Instead of this, Gilbert's plans were set aside. The fisheries were carried on from England, and laws were enacted forbidding the fishermen to settle in the island, as we shall see farther on in this history, and compelling them to return home each year as winter approached. For the benefit of a few greedy, selfish men the island was kept, for a long time, a mere fishing-station, and all the money made by fishing was spent in other lands, and the country left in a wilderness condition.

QUESTIONS FOR EXAMINATION ON CHAPTER IV.

1. Who were the first to engage in the Newfoundland fisheries? At what time? What place in Newfoundland was named by the Basques? Who discovered Conception Bay, and when? What number of vessels were employed in the fisheries in 1517, 1527, and 1578? How many were English?

2. Describe the voyage of Verazzani. When did he sail? What did France claim from his discoveries?

3. Who was Cartier? What discoveries did he make? What result followed to France?

4. Name other French explorers who followed Cartier. What did Acadia include? Who discovered the sources of the Mississippi? Who first sailed down its entire length? What claim did France make in consequence? Why was Louisiana so named?

5. Has Spain or France any possessions in the continent of America now?

6. On what did England's title to a portion of North America rest?

7. Who was Sir Humphrey Gilbert? Who was his half brother? What was his character? What opinion did he form of the Newfoundland fisheries and the best way of carrying them on?

8. Who gave him letters-patent? What jurisdiction did these give him?

9. Why did Raleigh not accompany Gilbert? What ships had Gilbert, and what tonnage were they? How many men?

10. What did he find in St. John's harbour? Give the date of his landing. How did he take possession of the island?

11. What ship did he send home? Describe the wreck of the "Delight." Why did Gilbert return to England?

12. Why did Gilbert refuse to leave the "Squirrel"? Describe the loss of this vessel. What were Gilbert's last words?

13. What vessel reached England? How was Sir Humphrey Gilbert's death such a loss to Newfoundland?

MAP QUESTIONS.

Where is Brittany? Normandy? The Basque provinces? Point out Port-aux-Basques. Where is St. Malo? Gaspé? Quebec? Montreal? Trace La Salle's voyage on the Mississippi. Where is Devonshire? Torbay? St. John's, Newfoundland? Cape Race? The Azores? Falmouth?

NOTES AND EXPLANATIONS. — CHAPTER IV.

Consumption of Fish. — The consumption of fresh and salted fish in Europe before the discovery of America, and for a long period afterwards, was immense. It must be remembered that all Europe, England included, was then Catholic; and during the fasts of the Church the pickled herring of Holland was the principal food. The foundations of Amsterdam were said to be laid on herring-bones. The Dutch became immensely wealthy by their monopoly of the herring-fisheries. In noblemen's families in England, at that period, retainers and servants lived on salt beef and mutton; but for three-fourths of the year on fish, with little or no vegetables. In the great Earl of Northumberland's establishment it is on record in their household book that "my lord and lady had for breakfast a quart of beer, as much wine, two pieces of saltfish, six red herrings, four white ones, and a dish of sprats." No wonder that Cabot's discovery of the Newfoundland fisheries created such a sensation and led to an excitement on the subject of fishing. Persons of the highest distinction took part in the fishing adventures of those days, and a rapid extension of the Bank and shore fishery followed on the part of France and England. Thus the enterprises of the hardy fishermen of both nations, to procure an article of food for the fast days of the Church, led to the most important political results. Even when England had become Protestant, laws were passed to promote the consumption of fish among the people, in order to encourage the fishing industries, especially those in American waters. In 1563, in the reign of Elizabeth, a law was passed which provided "that as well for the maintenance of shipping, the increase of fishermen and mariners, and the repairing of port-towns, as for the sparing of the fresh victual of the realm, it shall not be lawful for any one to eat flesh on Wednesdays and Saturdays, unless under the forfeiture of £3 for each offence, except in case of sickness and those of special licenses to be obtained." Other laws followed until there were one hundred and fifty-three days on which only fish could be eaten. The punishment for the violation of these laws was, for the first offence a fine of ten shillings and ten days' imprisonment; for the second, double these inflictions. No wonder fish was in great demand.

Francis I. — King of France from 1515 till 1547. His famous interview with Henry VIII., of England, on "the Field of the Cloth of Gold," took place in 1520. He was taken prisoner in the battle of Pavia, in 1525.

Jacques Cartier. — A native of St. Malo, a seaport in the northwest of France, on the north coast of the province of Bretagne. He was the discoverer of Canada and the St. Lawrence. He and Roberval met in 1542, in the harbour of St. John's, Newfoundland. Roberval was on his way to Canada; Cartier was on his way home to France. Roberval, as commander of the expedition, ordered Cartier to return to Canada; but he refused, and sailed for France. Roberval went on, built a fort on the St. Lawrence, and perished with his men, by cold and famine, during the following winter.

Samuel de Champlain, born at Brouage, a small seaport on the Bay of Biscay. He fought under Henry of Navarre, or Henry IV., the first king of the House of Bourbon. Being a favourite at court, he obtained command of an expedition to Canada, to explore and colonize. He was a man of noble character, courageous, disinterested, kind, and courteous. His remarkable exploits and labours belong to the history of Canada, in whose interests he toiled for thirty years, and of which he was the Father and Founder. He was appointed, at length, Governor of Canada, in 1633, and died two years after, universally lamented. Lake Champlain, of which he was the discoverer, bears his name.

Sir Humphrey Gilbert was a son of Sir Otho Gilbert, of Compton Castle, Torbay. His mother was a Champernoun, of purest Norman descent. Sir Otho had three sons by this lady, — John, Humphrey, and Adrian, — who all proved to be men of superior abilities. They were all three knighted by Elizabeth. Sir Otho died, and his widow married Walter Raleigh, a gentleman of ancient blood, but impoverished. To her second husband she bore a son whose fame was destined to be worldwide, and who was knighted as Sir Walter Raleigh by Elizabeth. Not many women could boast of being the mother of four such sons.

CHRONOLOGICAL SUMMARY.—CHAPTERS III. AND IV.

A.D.
1497. Vasco da Gama, a Portuguese navigator, doubled the Cape of Good Hope and reached India.
1509. Henry VIII. King of England.
1512. Florida discovered by De Leon.
1513. The Pacific Ocean discovered by Balboa.
1515. Francis I. King of France.
1519. Charles V. King of Spain and Emperor of Germany.
1520. Magellan's voyage round the globe.
1521. Mexico conquered by Cortes.
1524. North America coasted by Verazzani.
1531. Peru conquered by Pizarro.
1534. St. Lawrence discovered by Cartier.
1541. The Mississippi discovered by De Soto.
1552. Edmund Spenser born.
1558. Elizabeth Queen of England.
1556. Philip II. King of Spain.
1564. Shakespeare born.
1577. Drake's voyage round the world.
1588. Spanish Armada invaded England.
1589. Henry IV. (first Bourbon) King of France.

EMINENT MEN IN THE SIXTEENTH CENTURY.

Michael Angelo; Raffaelle; Sir Philip Sidney; Spenser; Shakespeare; Cervantes; Copernicus; Martin Luther; Cardinal Bellarmine; John Knox; Ignatius Loyola; Tycho Brahe.

CHAPTER V.

FISHERIES.

FROM 1583 TO 1615.

INCREASE OF THE ENGLISH COD-FISHERY. — GUY'S SETTLEMENT IN CONCEPTION BAY. — ITS FAILURE.

1. Though the voyage of Sir Humphrey Gilbert ended so disastrously to himself and others, it was far from being fruitless. It fixed the attention of Englishmen on Newfoundland and its valuable fisheries, and prepared the way for other enterprises designed to promote its settlement. Not only so, but Gilbert's attempt at colonization awoke in the minds of his countrymen that spirit of adventure which led them to plant colonies in New England, which have since grown into the great Republic of the United States.

2. Undeterred by the sad fate of Gilbert, his half-brother, Sir Walter Raleigh, obtained a patent from Queen Elizabeth for planting colonies in America. In 1584 he fitted out two ships and founded a colony, which he named Virginia, after the maiden queen. No colony can claim to date so far back, and hence it is often called "The Old Dominion." This gallant Englishman stands foremost among the colonizers of the New World. He undauntedly pursued these enterprises, and lavished his fortune on them. He diffused among his countrymen such a knowledge of America, and such an interest in its destinies, as bore abundant fruit, long after he was laid in the grave. No braver or more patriotic Englishman ever lived. No greater disgrace attached to the name of James I., of England, than the act of sending to the block, in his old age, and after twelve years' imprisonment, Sir Walter Raleigh, the gallant soldier, the accomplished scholar, the far-seeing statesman, the persevering colonizer. It was not, however, till thirteen years after Raleigh's first effort that the first permanent English colony was formed in Virginia, in 1620, under a charter from James I. It was planted at Jamestown, on the shores of Chesapeake Bay.

SIR FRANCIS DRAKE.

3. For twenty-seven years after the failure of Gilbert's expedition no fresh attempt was made to found a colony in Newfoundland. War between England and Spain broke out in 1584. The bold sea-rover, Sir Francis Drake, was despatched with a small squadron to Newfoundland, where he made prizes of a number of Portuguese vessels, laden with fish and oil, and carried them to England. The attention of English adventurers was once more turned to Newfoundland. There is a record of one Richard Apsham,

who, in 1593, fitted out two vessels for the purpose of taking walruses, on the south-west coast, where, at that time, these animals were plentiful. Four years later some London merchants fitted out two armed vessels, which, after fishing some time on the Banks, encountered some French and Spanish vessels off the southern shore. After a sharp contest the English vessels captured the others, and carried one of them to Gravesend, with a valuable cargo of fish and oil. One of the English ships, however, was wrecked on Cape Breton.

4. Meantime the shores of Newfoundland were resorted to by the fishermen of various nations, who took fish in its waters, and used its harbours and coves for curing and drying them. In 1577 there were 100 Spanish and 50 Portuguese vessels thus employed; but they rapidly diminished in numbers, and, in a short time, withdrew almost entirely from these fisheries. The wealth to be acquired in the gold regions of South America soon proved a stronger attraction to the Spaniards than this sea-harvest, which could only be gathered amid toils and dangers. Portugal, too, preferred colonization in South America, and the acquisition of wealth in the mines of Brazil. Thus the Newfoundland fisheries were left to the English and French. In 1577 the French had 150 vessels employed, and prosecuted the fisheries with great vigour and success. On the accession of Henry IV., the first Bourbon, the cod-fishery was placed under the protection of the government, and was regarded as being of great national importance, and such it has been ever since.

5. The English, who were later in commencing this industry, soon gained rapidly on their rivals, the French. During the ten years which followed the death of Gilbert, ending in 1593, the progress of the English fishery in

Newfoundland was so great that Sir Walter Raleigh declared, in the House of Commons, "it was the stay and support of the west counties of England." In the year 1600 it is known that 200 English ships went to Newfoundland, and that they employed, as catchers on board, and curers on shore, quite 10,000 men and boys. Sir William Monson, an Englishman who wrote in 1610, declared that since the island was taken possession of the fisheries had been worth £100,000 annually to British subjects. This was an immense sum in those days. He further said that these fisheries had greatly increased the number of England's ships and mariners. The ships left England in March for the fishing-grounds, and returned in September. The fishermen passed their winters in England, idly spending their summer earnings.

6. It is not wonderful, under such circumstances, when Newfoundland was so prominently before the minds of Englishmen, that a second effort should be made to plant a colony on its shores. In 1609 John Guy, a merchant, and afterwards mayor of Bristol, published a pamphlet, in which he pointed out the advantages of colonizing the island. It was evident that much time and money were wasted in carrying on the fisheries from England. To persons of broad, liberal views it was clear that the right method was to hold out inducements to fishermen to live permanently near the fishing-grounds, — the plan proposed by Sir Humphrey Gilbert. Guy's pamphlet made such a deep impression on the public mind that a company was formed to carry out the enterprise it suggested. Several noblemen having influence at the court of James I. took part in this undertaking. Among these were the celebrated Lord Bacon, who was then Solicitor General; Lord Northampton, Keeper of the Seals; Sir Francis Tanfield,

Chief Baron of the Exchequer; Sir Daniel Donu, and other noblemen and gentlemen to the number of fifty. The importance of the island as a site for a colony did not escape the wide-ranging eye of Lord Bacon, who declared that " its fisheries were more valuable than all the mines of Peru." This judgment has been amply confirmed by time and experience. To this company James I., by letters-patent, dated April, 1610, made a grant of all that part of Newfoundland which lies between Cape Bonavista and Cape St. Mary.

7. The enterprise, thus favourably commenced, was not successful. Guy was appointed governor, and, with a considerable number of colonists, landed at Mosquito Cove, near Harbour Grace, on the north shore of Conception Bay. Here temporary habitations were erected. By kindly and prudent measures he conciliated the native Indians, and secured their friendship. Little is known regarding the history of this settlement, which, according to Whitbourne's account, continued for four or five years in a fairly prosperous condition. For some unexplained reason Guy and some of the colonists returned to England, and those who remained moved to other localities. It is not improbable that piracy was the cause of the failure. In 1612 Peter Easton, a noted pirate, with ten well-appointed ships, made himself complete master of the seas, and levied a general contribution on vessels employed in fishing. He made a descent on Conception Bay, and seized a hundred of the fishermen there, and carried them off to man his own fleet. It is not unlikely that the infant settlement of Guy was so harassed and plundered by this freebooter that it was broken up.

8. The year 1613 is memorable as that in which the first child of European parents was born in Newfoundland.

QUESTIONS FOR EXAMINATION ON CHAPTER V.

1. What important results followed from Sir Humphrey Gilbert's voyage to Newfoundland?

2. Who founded the Colony of Virginia, and in what year? What was the character of Sir Walter Raleigh? What was his fate? When and where was the first permanent settlement formed in Virginia?

3. When did Sir Francis Drake visit Newfoundland, and what did he do? For what purpose did Richard Apsham send vessels? What occurred in 1597?

4. When were Spanish and Portuguese fishing-vessels most numerous in Newfoundland waters? Why did they withdraw? How many French vessels were fishing in 1577?

5. What shows the increase of English fishing-vessels? What did Sir Walter Raleigh say of the value of these fisheries? What did Sir William Molson say of them? What time did the English fishermen leave home and return?

6. Who was John Guy? What steps did he take to establish a colony in the island? Who joined him? What did Lord Bacon say of the fisheries? What was the date of Guy's patent? What was the extent of the grant?

7. Where did Guy commence a settlement? How long did it continue? What was the probable cause of its failure?

8. What is the year 1613 noted for?

MAP QUESTIONS.

Where is Virginia? Jamestown? Chesapeake Bay? What State is on the south of Virginia? Where is Gravesend? Brazil? Point out Mosquito Cove.

NOTES AND EXPLANATIONS.—CHAPTER V.

Sir Walter Raleigh's death on the scaffold was a very pathetic scene. He first knelt down and prayed; then he arose and examined the block. "Show me the axe," he said to the executioner. Touching the edge with his finger and kissing the blade, he said, "This gives me no fear. It is a sharp and fair medicine to cure me of all my diseases." He laid his head on the block, and when the headsman, much moved, hesitated to strike, Raleigh said, "What dost thou fear? Strike, man, strike!" He lay quite still, and his lips were seen to move in prayer. At two blows his head was severed from his body. Thus was put to death, at the age of sixty-six, a brave man, who had, in his day, but few equals.

Virginia.—Tobacco and the potato were brought to England by Raleigh, and their use in Europe dates from his time. So profitable was the growth of tobacco in Virginia that for a time the very streets of Jamestown were planted with it. Everything was paid for in tobacco, as there was little or no money. Salaries of clergy, taxes, debts, were paid in tobacco. Ninety respectable young women were sent out by the company from England, and whoever took one of them for a wife must pay a hundred pounds of tobacco. If a woman was convicted of slander her husband had to pay a fine of one hundred pounds of tobacco.

Lord Bacon.—Born in 1561, he rose to be Lord Chancellor in the reign of James I. His is the greatest name connected with Newfoundland's colonizers. He was the apostle of experimental philosophy, of whom Macaulay says: "Turn where you will, the trophies of his mighty intellect are in view." His greatest works were "The Advancement of Learning" and "The Novum Organon," the influence of which was immense. His intellectual grandeur has rarely been surpassed. Unhappily, he yielded to the corrupting influences of his time, and tarnished his fair fame by accepting bribes in his high judicial office. For this he was sentenced to pay a fine of £40,000, which was afterwards remitted. He spent his closing years in scientific pursuits, and died in 1626.

CHAPTER VI.

FROM 1615 TO 1655.

WHITBOURNE'S COMMISSION.

SIR GEORGE CALVERT'S CHARTER. — FIRST ARRIVAL OF EMIGRANTS FROM IRELAND. — SIR DAVID KIRKE'S ARRIVAL.

1. WE now come to an important period in the history of the island, and one which marks its rising importance. In 1615 Captain Richard Whitbourne, mariner, of Exmouth, Devonshire, received a commission from the Admiralty of England to proceed to Newfoundland, for the purpose of establishing order among the fishing population, and remedying certain abuses which had grown up there. The appointment of Whitbourne shows that the trade and fisheries of the island were now chiefly in the hands of the English, as he could not exercise such jurisdiction except over British subjects. On his arrival at St. John's, he summoned a court, empanelled juries, and heard the complaints of no less than 170 masters of English vessels, regarding injuries to the fisheries and trade of the island. He found that there were, besides the vessels of foreign flags, 250 English ships employed in the fisheries. His courts and juries were the first attempts at the establishment of law and order in the New World, under the authority of England. These facts show in what a flourishing condition was the English cod-fishery at this early date.

2. Already fixed settlements had commenced, which gradually extended from Torbay (originally Thornebay),

six miles north of St. John's, to Cape Race (originally Raze). To connect these settlements, scattered over such an extent of coast, with St. John's, the settlers cut paths through the woods. Vessels arriving at St. John's supplied them with necessaries, in exchange for the produce of the fisheries.

3. In 1622 Whitbourne returned to England, where he published a book, called "A Discourse and Discovery of Newfoundland." In this book he spoke highly of the climate, soil, and fisheries, and strongly urged his countrymen to colonize it. King James ordered a copy of this book to be sent to every parish in the kingdom. The Archbishops of Canterbury and York issued a letter recommending it to the notice of the people, in order to induce Englishmen to emigrate to Newfoundland. Thus, 263 years ago, Newfoundland was a name on the lips of Englishmen, and was probably more widely known than it came to be long afterwards, when it was misrepresented and decried by interested persons, from selfish motives, and treated as a place of little importance.

4. We now come to notice the best-regulated effort yet made to plant a colony in Newfoundland. This was carried out under the guidance of Sir George Calvert, afterwards Lord Baltimore. He was a Roman Catholic gentleman of Yorkshire, who had been knighted by James I., and appointed by him one of the secretaries of state. He was a man of intelligence, lofty integrity, and possessed of great capacity for business. From the king he obtained, in 1623, a patent conveying to him the lordship of the whole southern peninsula of Newfoundland. He named it Avalon, from the ancient name of Glastonbury, Somersetshire, where Christianity is said to have been first preached in England. One of his objects was to provide a refuge for his co-religionists,

of the Roman Catholic faith, who were suffering from the persecuting spirit then unhappily prevalent, more or less, among all religious bodies.

5. Sir George Calvert selected Ferryland, forty miles north of Cape Race, as the site of his colony. Here he built a noble mansion, in which he resided for several years. He used great care in selecting colonists of the right stamp, and endeavoured to promote among them habits of industry and economy. He also erected a strong fort for their protection, and large granaries and storehouses. On this settlement he expended £30,000, — a large sum in those days. For

LORD BALTIMORE.

a time things seemed to prosper. Reinforcements of colonists continued to arrive, and supplies of stores and implements. But the soil around Ferryland was unfavourable for cultivation. The French, who had now got a footing in Newfoundland, in several places, and who were at war with the English, harassed his settlement with repeated attacks.

6. Wearied by these adverse circumstances he at length gave up his plantation and returned to England. From Charles I. he obtained a patent of the country now called Maryland. Before his patent had passed the necessary forms Lord Baltimore died in London, in 1632; but a new one was issued to his son, Cecil, who succeeded to his honours, and founded the city of Baltimore, in Maryland. Before his death the first Lord Baltimore drew up a charter for the Maryland colony, which showed that in wisdom, liberality, and statesmanship he was far ahead of his age. The Catholic Lord Baltimore was the first to establish a constitution which embodied the principle of complete liberty of conscience, the equality of all Christian sects, together with popular institutions, on the broad basis of freedom. Thus he is deservedly ranked among the wisest and best law-givers of all ages. Most of the colonists he brought to Newfoundland remained to increase the resident population.

7. The first arrival of emigrants from Ireland took place soon after the departure of Lord Baltimore. Viscount Falkland was then Lord Lieutenant of Ireland. He sent out a body of settlers from that country to increase the small population of Newfoundland. These, at a later date, were followed by many more. In this way it came about that the population of the island was composed of English and Irish settlers and their descendants; and, at one time, the Saxon and Celtic elements were in almost equal proportions. It is not improbable that the disturbed condition of Ireland led a number of its people, from time to time, to seek a happier home and greater freedom on the shores of Newfoundland.

8. The next charter for the settlement of the island was given to Sir David Kirke, who arrived in 1638.

This brave sea-captain had won high honours in warlike operations against the French in Canada. He had captured a French fleet at Gaspé; made a clean sweep of all the French settlements in Canada and Acadia, and taken Quebec. He was knighted for his bravery by Charles I., who also made a grant in his favour of the whole island of Newfoundland. He took up his abode at Ferryland, in the house built by Lord Baltimore. Sir David governed wisely, and used every effort to promote the settlement of the country. Much success attended his efforts. But the civil war in England, between Charles and the Parliament, now commenced. Kirke was a stanch loyalist, and all his possessions in Newfoundland were confiscated by the victorious Commonwealth. By the aid of Claypole, Cromwell's son-in-law, he was at length reinstated in his possessions, and, returning to Ferryland, died there, in 1655, at the age of fifty-six.

CECIL, SECOND LORD BALTIMORE.

QUESTIONS FOR EXAMINATION ON CHAPTER VI.

1. When did Captain Whitbourne arrive, and for what purpose was he sent? What does his appointment show? In what state did he find the fisheries?

2. Where were there fixed settlements at this time?

3. What did Whitbourne do on his return to England? What do you know of his book on the Island?

4. Who was Sir George Calvert? What was his character? What was the date of his patent and what the extent of his grant? What is the origin of the name Avalon? What object had Calvert in view?

5. Where did he settle? What did he do to secure prosperity to his settlement, and how much money did he expend? What caused failure?

6. Where did Calvert go on leaving? What colony was founded by his son? What is the constitution of Maryland noted for?

7. When did the first Irish emigrants arrive?

8. What is the date of Kirke's settlement? What led to his coming? Give an account of his colony. Where did he die and when?

MAP QUESTIONS.

Where is Devonshire? Exmouth? Glastonbury? Ferryland? Maryland? Gaspé?

NOTES AND EXPLANATIONS. — CHAPTER VI.

Captain Whitbourne was connected with the trade of Newfoundland for forty years, and had formed a high opinion of the capabilities of the country. His memory deserves to be held in lasting respect for the services he rendered in drawing attention to the island, and urging its colonization. Like most seamen he had his superstitions, and believed firmly in the existence of mermaids. In his book he gives an amusing account of seeing one of these fabulous creatures in the harbour of St. John's. He says it came swimming towards him, "looking cheerfully into his face," the face, nose, eyes, and forehead beautiful as a woman's, with "blue streaks" about the head like hair. This fascinating creature came so boldly and swiftly towards the gallant captain that he thought she meant to spring ashore to him. He had commanded a ship, and fought bravely against the Spanish Armada, but he thought it prudent to run when he saw the mermaid approaching. Perhaps he thought she intended to carry him off to her sea-caves. The mermaid then swam away, "often looking back towards me;" the back and shoulders were "white and smooth as the back of a man." "This," says the captain, "was, I suppose, a mermaid or merman; but I leave it to others to judge."

There can be no doubt that the honest captain had seen a seal disporting in the waters of the harbour, in the haze of the morning, and his excited imagination did the rest.

Ferryland is thirty-five miles south of St. John's. Avalon was the ancient name of Glastonbury. The old Roman town of Verulam occupied the site there of what was afterwards St. Albans Abbey. Calvert, to perpetuate these memories, called his province Avalon, and his town Verulam, which was corrupted first into Ferulam and then into Ferryland. Bonnycastle, however, says its original name was Fore-Island, which is applicable to the locality. This was corrupted into Forriland, and then into Ferriland, which name it bore in the days of Calvert, as it is written so in a letter from the place dated 1622.

The changes and corruptions of the original French names are often curious. Bay of Bulls is a corruption of the French words *Baie des Boules*. Catalina harbour, from St. Catherine's, was originally named by the Spaniards Catalina, being the musical Spanish name for *Catherine*, like the Irish Kathleen. The French *Baie d'Espoir* (Bay of Hope) is now, by corruption of the name, Bay Despair. *Baie de Lièvre* is Bay Deliver. *Baie le Diable* has become Jabbouls. *Lance au Diable* is Nancy Jobble. *Baie de Vieux*, or Old Man's Bay, is Bay-the-View. *Baie d'Aviron* is now Aberoon. Twillingate was originally *Toulinguet*. *Tasse à l'arpent* is Tostleojohn. *Beau Bois* is Boboy.

The presence of the French in Newfoundland is attested by countless names of places, such as Notre Dame Bay; Cape Freehel (now Freels); Plaisance or Placentia, on account of its beautiful situation; St. Jude's (now Cape Judy); Trepassey, the Bay of the Trepasses, or All-Souls; Audierne (now Oderin); Cape de Raz, or Capo Raco, bare Cape (Cape Race); Cape Ray (Raye), or Split Cape, from its appearance at sea; Burgeo, La Poile, La Hune, Rose Blanche, and numberless places on the southern shore. Fermosa, now Fermeuse, the beautiful, and Renews, the rocky, must have been named by the Portuguese.

CHAPTER VII.

FROM 1600 TO 1650.

CONTEMPORARY EVENTS.

PROGRESS OF THE NEW ENGLAND COLONIES. — FRENCH COLONIZATION IN CANADA AND ACADIA. —CONFLICT BETWEEN ENGLAND AND FRANCE IN NORTH AMERICA.

1. We must now pause for a moment, in following the fortunes of Newfoundland, in order to learn what Englishmen had been doing, during the half century from 1600 to 1650, in planting colonies on the shores of North America; and how the French progressed in colonizing Canada and Acadia. This is necessary in order to understand thoroughly the history of Newfoundland.

We have already seen how the first permanent English colony was formed at Jamestown, in Virginia, in 1607. At first it did not prosper, and several times it was on the point of extinction. At length, however, emigrants of a better sort found their way to Virginia, and the colony began to grow, and several other towns arose. The early settlers found tobacco in extensive use among the Indians. When introduced into England it speedily obtained favour. The Virginian settlers soon found the cultivation of it a source of great profit. In eighty years Virginia numbered 50,000 inhabitants.

2. The 21st of December, 1620, was a memorable day in the history of the New World. On that day a little band of one hundred, called afterwards " the Pilgrim Fathers," landed from the *Mayflower*, on

Plymouth Rock,—a granite boulder on the shore of Cape Cod Bay, which is still reverently preserved by their descendants. They had fled from tyranny and persecution in England, first to Holland, and then they determined to seek for a home and freedom amid the great forests of New England. They had terrible hardships and difficulties to encounter, but they bravely surmounted them all. Nine years after, in 1629, five vessels sailed into Salem harbour, with another band of emigrants on board, direct from England; and the next year eight hundred more arrived. These were "Puritans," seeking freedom of worship and safety from persecution. They founded the towns of Salem and Boston; and the new colony was called Massachusetts Bay. Afterwards Plymouth colony united with this one, under the name of Massachusetts,—an Indian word, signifying, it is said, " Blue Hills."

3. These were the first of the New England colonies: others speedily followed. Rhode Island was established in 1636; Connecticut in 1638; then New Hampshire and Vermont. Twenty-four years after the landing of the "Pilgrims" the Dutch discovered the Hudson river, and built a trading-post on Manhattan Island. They called the whole territory along the river " New Netherlands," and founded a settlement named " New Amsterdam," where now stands the great city of New York. The colony prospered. At length, in 1664, certain English ships of war entered the bay. New Amsterdam surrendered; the whole colony passed under British rule, and in honour of the Duke of York, afterwards James II., was named New York. The southern portion of the territory was named New Jersey.

4. Thus rapidly was the work of colonization carried on, while in Newfoundland so many efforts at settle-

ment proved unsuccessful. Pennsylvania, North and South Carolina, and Georgia were founded at a later date. These early New England colonists were men of brave hearts and strong arms, possessed of a free, bold spirit, with ability and determination to manage their own affairs. They came of their own free choice to make a home for themselves, and their rise to strength and greatness was rapid. One noble purpose these colonists never lost sight of was the education of their children. They knew that no success could attend their efforts if their children were allowed to grow up in ignorance. One of their earliest efforts was to establish everywhere common schools, in which every child should receive a good education. We need not wonder that colonies planted by such men soon attained a robust growth. When, in 1774, the American Revolution began, the thirteen colonies had a population of between two and three millions. It is not wonderful that they won their independence. At that time England had but 6,000,000, Scotland 1,000,000, and Ireland 2,000,000 inhabitants.

5. Meantime, let us see what progress the French were making in Canada. We have already seen how they were led, by taking part in the Newfoundland fisheries, to take possession of Canada and Acadia. Here they determined to establish a dominion worthy of the great name of France. No expense was spared to promote the growth of colonies, which would give them a firm hold on these magnificent possessions. Able and wise governors were appointed; soldiers for defence were furnished; food was supplied in seasons of scarcity.

In this way the dominion of France gradually extended itself along the St. Lawrence, amid ceaseless and destructive wars with the native Indians. Quebec and Montreal were founded. From the great lakes the French pushed their discoveries and explorations down the Mississippi to the Gulf of Mexico, and claimed the whole territory drained by it and its tributaries. Soon they came in collision with the New England colonists, who were extending themselves northward, and wanted to secure for themselves the valuable Canadian fur trade. At a later date the two nations also met in the valley of the Ohio, where the French prohibited the English colonists from trading. Bloody and wasteful wars were carried on, and both sides endeavoured to secure the assistance of the Indians. The conflict thus commenced went on for a century and a half, during the greater part of which time England and France were at war. England assisted her colonies in carrying on war against the French, with the view of expelling them altogether from the American continent. The French fought with great bravery in defence of their possessions, but in vain. Gradually their power was weakened. One after another their strongholds were captured; and at length their last battle was fought on the Heights of Abraham, in 1759, and Quebec was taken by General Wolfe. This was one of the decisive battles of the world; and after it the white flag of France no longer waved on the continent of America.

6. It is not difficult to see how the French were driven from Canada. They have never been successful as colonizers. In the New World they spent their strength mainly in military adventures, in discoveries, and trading operations. They did little in cultivating the soil and making permanent homes for themselves. They carried the feudal institutions of old France into the Canadian wilderness, and the land was parcelled out

among a few nobles, who oppressed the people. Monopolies of trade were given to favoured individuals. Few Frenchmen emigrated voluntarily to Canada, and the colony remained feeble and unprogressive. When the New England colonists had grown to be over a million strong, the French in the valley of the St. Lawrence numbered only sixty-five thousand. These could not stand before the sturdy English colonists, backed by the military resources of the mother-country. Great names adorn the history of New France, such as Champlain, De Monts, La Tour, La Salle, Frontenac, Montcalm. These men well sustained the fame of their country, and employed all their genius and bravery in establishing her power. The self-devotion and zeal of the Jesuit fathers, in prosecuting their missions among the Indians, awaken our admiration. But all failed in giving France a permanent hold on Canada.

QUESTIONS FOR EXAMINATION ON CHAPTER VII.

1. What industry was carried on by the early Virginia settlers? Did they increase?
2. When did the Pilgrim Fathers arrive? Where did they land? Why did they leave home? Where did the Puritans land? What towns did they found?
3. Give the dates of Rhode Island, Connecticut, New Hampshire, and Vermont. Who first settled in New York? When did it become an English possession? What was the origin of the name, New York?
4. What other colonies followed? What kind of men were the New England colonists? How did they show their regard for education? What was the population of these colonies at the time of the American Revolution?
5. What led the French to occupy Canada? What efforts did they make to settle it? Describe their progress. Where did they come in collision with the English colonists? What was the issue of the conflict?
6. Why did the French fail to settle and hold Canada? Point out the weak points in their system of settlement. Mention some of their greatest representatives in Canada.

MAP QUESTIONS.

Where did the "Pilgrim Fathers" land? Point out, on the map, Boston, Salem, Plymouth, New York, Hudson River, States of Connecticut, New Hampshire, Rhode Island, Pennsylvania, the Carolinas, Georgia, Quebec, Montreal. Trace the course of the Ohio River.

CHAPTER VIII.

FROM 1655 TO 1697.

THE FRENCH IN NEWFOUNDLAND.

PLACENTIA FOUNDED. — FRENCH EFFORTS TO GET POSSESSION OF THE ISLAND. — EXPEDITION OF D'IBERVILLE. — TREATY OF RYSWICK. — ITS EFFECT ON NEWFOUNDLAND.

1. The great events referred to in the last chapter were closely connected with the history of Newfoundland, and greatly influenced the fortunes of the colony. In carrying out their plans for founding an empire in the New World, the French statesmen were eager for the conquest of Newfoundland. The possession of the island they knew would enable them to control the fisheries, and also to command the narrow entrance to the St. Lawrence and their possessions in Canada. Hence, they never ceased their efforts to obtain a footing in the island; and their presence and encroachments were a constant source of annoyance to the English and Irish settlers.

2. In 1635 the French obtained permission from England to dry fish on the shores of Newfoundland, on payment of a duty of five per cent. on the produce. In 1660 the French founded Placentia, on the southern coast. The entrance to this beautiful and commodious harbor is a narrow strait, which they defended by the erection of Fort St. Louis, a strong fortification that stood at the foot of a rocky height. A French lieutenant-governor was nominated to take command and re-

PLACENTIA.

side here. In 1675 Charles II. was persuaded by Louis XIV. to give up the duty of five per cent. hitherto paid as an acknowledgment that the island belonged to England. From this time the French became bolder and more determined in extending their settlements, especially along the southern shore, where many of the places to this day bear the French names given by them.

3. When war broke out between England and France, on the accession of William III. to the throne, one of the reasons assigned in the royal declaration of war, was that the French had been, of late, making unwarrantable encroachments in Newfoundland. To check these, Commodore Williams was despatched, in 1692, with a squadron, to seize Placentia. On arriving he found that a strong boom had been thrown across the entrance of the harbour, and that he had three well-armed forts to attack. After a brisk cannonade, he withdrew, finding the place too strong to be captured with the force under his command.

4. It was now the turn of the French to become the assailants; and their determined efforts to seize Newfoundland were crowned with a short-lived success. In 1696 Chevalier Nesmond, a French commander with a strong squadron, was ordered to drive the English out of Newfoundland, and then to destroy Boston and the neighbouring settlements. He arrived at Placentia, and from thence made a descent on St. John's, which was at this time defended by several forts, and held by a garrison. Thirty-four English ships were then lying in the harbour. Nesmond's attack was successfully repulsed, and he returned to France without accomplishing anything.

5. But the French persevered in their designs of conquest. Later in the same year a more formidable

expedition was prepared. There was then in Canada a famous captain called D'Iberville (pronounced *Dee-bair-véel*), who was much employed in harassing the English settlements. He had just distinguished himself by his skill and bravery in capturing Fort William Henry, which had been built by the government of Massachusetts, at Pemaquid, east of the river Kennebec. He was then ordered to join Brouillan, Governor of Placentia, who had a number of vessels under his command. The combined force was to effect the conquest of Newfoundland.

6. Before his arrival, Brouillan had sailed to attack Ferryland. On his way he met a solitary English man-of-war, which he chased into the Bay of Bulls. Captain Cleasby was its commander, and he determined to defend his vessel to the last. The gallant captain placed all his guns on the broadside next the enemy, and fought furiously till his vessel took fire, when he escaped to the shore. The Frenchmen followed him, and he and his men had to surrender. Ferryland was then destroyed by Brouillan. D'Iberville now joined him, and a strong body of the French advanced through the woods, and made an attack on St. John's, in the rear. The garrison was feeble, and in want of military stores and provisions. They could make but a faint resistance, and St. John's was captured and burned. The garrison and principal inhabitants were allowed two ships to carry them to England. The rest made their way to Carbonear and Bonavista. D'Iberville then followed up his successes by destroying all the English settlements on the eastern coast. Carbonear, however, where the descendants of Guy's settlers had established themselves, made a gallant resistance, and beat off the enemy. Bonavista, also, was too strong for him, and

made an equally successful resistance. The whole of Newfoundland, with the exception of these two places, was now in the hands of the French.

7. As soon as the news of the loss of Newfoundland reached England strong preparations were made for driving out the invaders. Before anything effectual could be done the war between England and France was brought to a close by the treaty of Ryswick, signed on the 20th September, 1697.

8. By the seventh article of this treaty England and France agreed to mutually restore all their possessions in North America which had changed hands during the war. Thus the French were reinstated in all they had lost, and all the bloodshed and sufferings of eight years decided nothing as to who should be masters of North America.

9. The treaty, in its effects, was most injurious to Newfoundland. It left the island, as at the commencement of the war, divided between the English and French; so that, if war should be renewed, the English settlements were as liable as before to be harassed by the attacks of the French. St. John's, and the other settlements which the French had seized, were given up. But their claims on Placentia, and all other positions on the south-west coast, were recognized and confirmed. The consequence was frequent hostilities and renewed efforts on the part of the French to get possession of the whole island, so that they were not shaken off for some years to come.

QUESTIONS FOR EXAMINATION ON CHAPTER VIII.

1. Why were the French so eager to get possession of Newfoundland?

2. What privilege did the French obtain in Newfoundland in 1635? When was Placentia founded? What fort was erected? What gave the French a greater hold on the island?

3. Who was sent to check French encroachments, and what did he do?

4. When did Nesmond invade Newfoundland, and what did he accomplish?

5. What orders were given to D'Iberville?

6. Describe his movement. What occurred at Bay of Bulls? What was the fate of St. John's? What two places resisted the French?

7. By what treaty was the war ended, and when?

8. What were some of its articles?

9. How did the treaty of Ryswick injure Newfoundland?

NOTES AND EXPLANATIONS. — CHAPTER VIII.

Ryswick. — A town in Holland, three miles from the Hague. In the royal palace here the treaty of peace was signed in 1697. The parties to it were England, France, Spain, Holland, and Germany. By it Louis XIV. acknowledged William III. lawful king of Great Britain and Ireland.

Placentia, on the bay of that name, on the southern coast, eighty miles from St. John's.

Bay of Bulls, eighteen miles south of St. John's.

CHAPTER IX.

FROM 1654 TO 1729.

CONDITION OF THE EARLY SETTLERS.

SLOW PROGRESS OF THE COLONY. — ITS CAUSE. — UNJUST LAWS. — TYRANNY BY ACT OF PARLIAMENT. — THE FISHING ADMIRALS. — OPPRESSION OF THE WEAK. — APPOINTMENT OF THE FIRST GOVERNOR.

1. While the population of the New England colonies was increasing rapidly, that of Newfoundland made very slow progress, though its settlement was of much earlier date. In 1654, seventy-one years after the arrival of Sir Humphrey Gilbert, the island contained a population of only 350 families, or about 1,750 persons. These were distributed in fifteen small settlements along the eastern shore. The principal of them were Torbay, Quidi Vidi, St. John's, Bay of Bulls, Ferryland, Renewse, Aquaforte. Twenty years later, in 1680, the resident population was 2,280. In eighteen years more, these had only increased to 2,640, this being their number in the year 1698. It must be remembered that, in addition to these, there was a large floating population of many thousands who frequented the shores during summer, to carry on the fisheries, but left for their homes at the approach of winter. In 1626 Devonshire alone sent 150 vessels to the cod-fishery.

2. But why, it may be asked, was the settlement of the island so slow? The climate was healthy, the soil repaid cultivation, the fisheries were most productive. Out of the many thousands who visited it how came it

that so few took up their permanent abode in the island?

There was a very sufficient reason for this, which we must now explain. So far as the English were concerned, the fisheries had been carried on by merchants, ship-owners, and traders who resided in the west of England. They sent out their ships and fishing-crews to Newfoundland early in the summer. The fish caught were salted and dried ashore. When winter approached the fishermen took their departure for England, carrying with them whatever portion of the fish had not been previously shipped for foreign markets. These English " merchant-adventurers," as they were called, found that it was for their interest to discourage the settlement of the country, as they wished to retain its harbours and coves for the use of their own fishing captains and servants, while engaged in curing and drying the fish. They got, at length, to think that the whole island was their own, and that any one who settled there was an interloper who should be driven away. They actually thought it right to keep an island larger than Ireland in a wilderness condition, in order that they might use its shores for drying their fish, and enjoy, in their own country, all the riches thus gathered.

3. But, in spite of all their efforts, a few hardy, adventurous persons began to form little settlements along the shores. The island had strong attractions for them, and they wanted to make homes for themselves, and combine cultivation of the land with fishing. The fishing-merchants and ship-owners took the alarm, and went to war with these settlers, determined to root them out, or, at all events, to keep their numbers as small as possible. Being wealthy capitalists they had great influence with the successive English governments of those

days, while the poor settlers had none. They were able to persuade the English statesmen and people that the fisheries would be ruined if a resident population should be allowed to grow up in the island, and the fisheries would no longer be a nursery of seamen for the navy. Further, they misled the public by representing the island as hopelessly barren, and, in regard to its soil and climate, unfit for human habitation.

4. In this way it came about that unjust and injurious laws were enacted by the English government, to prevent the settlement of the island, and to keep it forever in the degraded condition of a stage for drying fish. These laws forbade any one to go to Newfoundland as a settler, and ordained that all fishermen should return to England at the close of each fishing season. Masters of vessels were compelled to give bonds of £100, binding them to bring back each year such persons as they took out. Settlement within six miles of the coast was prohibited under heavy penalties. No one could cultivate or enclose the smallest piece of ground, or even repair a house, without license, which was rarely granted. This oppressive policy was maintained for more than a hundred years.

5. Notwithstanding these hardships and discouragements the sturdy settlers held their ground, and slowly but steadily increased in numbers. Between them and their oppressors a bitter antipathy sprang up, and it is not wonderful that it should have been so. There must have been among these settlers a manly, independent spirit. Had there not been among them men possessing much vigour of character and solid worth, they could not have carried on the contest so bravely against the fishing capitalists, and at last conquered them, and won their freedom. The conflict, however, was very trying, and

greatly retarded the progress of the colony, entailing terrible sufferings on men who were kept outside the pale of law, and without any civilizing influences. Finding their own fishery declining, while that carried on by the settlers was increasing, in 1670, the merchant-adventurers applied to the Lords of Trade and Plantations, and declared that unless the settlers were removed the fisheries would be destroyed. These Lords of Trade immediately sent out Sir John Berry, a naval officer, with orders to drive out the fishermen and burn their dwellings.

6. This barbarous edict was not revoked for six years. Though it was not strictly carried into effect, owing to the humane spirit of Sir John Berry, yet it gave the mercantile monopolists such an advantage that, soon after, they had 270 vessels and 11,000 men engaged in the fisheries. When the decree to burn and drive away was recalled, strict orders were given that no further emigration to the doomed island should be allowed. At length the Lords of Trade relaxed so far as to allow one thousand persons to reside in Newfoundland, as they might be useful in building boats and fishing stages, and taking care of property. The repressive policy reached its height when a certain Major Elford, lieutenant-governor at St. John's, very strongly urged the ministers of the day "to allow no woman to land in the island, and that means should be adopted to remove those who were there." It does not appear that any one tried to carry out this sweeping proposal.

7. As years rolled on, though the settlers were increasing in numbers and importance, they were as much as ever at the tender mercies of the merchants. One of the enactments of the notable Star Chamber, in the reign of Charles I., was, that if a person in Newfound-

land killed another, or stole the value of forty shillings, the offender was to be sent to England, and, on conviction of either offence, to be hanged. Another law was that the master of the first ship entering a harbour was to be admiral for the season, and magistrate of the district, with unlimited power to decide all questions regarding property and all other disputes. Thus arose government by the Fishing Admirals, perhaps the most absurd and tyrannical pretence at the administration of justice ever put in practice.

8. In 1698, in the reign of William III., this arrangement was confirmed and extended in an act passed by the British parliament. In this statute, which long obstructed all improvement in the country, it was ordained that the master of a vessel arriving first in a harbour was to be admiral for the season, and was allowed to take as much of the beach as he chose, for his own use. The masters of the second and third vessels arriving at the same harbour were to be vice-admiral and rear-admiral, with similar privileges. No attention was paid to the qualifications of these admirals. The first rude, ignorant skipper who made a short passage was absolute ruler for the season. They were the servants of the merchants, and therefore personally interested in questions of property that arose. They were the enemies of the poor residents, whom they wanted to trample out.

9. The triumph of the merchants over their fellow-subjects in this lone isle was now as complete as that of a warrior who storms a city. Their servants, the Fishing Admirals, took possession of the best fishing-stations, drove out the inhabitants from their own houses, gardens, and fishing-grounds; took bribes when determining cases, and carried on, for long years, a sys-

tem of robbery and oppression. All accounts agree in representing them as at once knaves and tyrants, though no doubt there were individual exceptions.

10. In vain did the resident people, groaning under the lash of these petty tyrants, petition the Lords of Trade, and lay before them their grievances. The merchants were able to get their petitions thrown aside with contempt. Again and again they asked for the appointment of a governor to regulate the affairs of the island. That, of all others, was a measure the merchants and ship-owners dreaded. It might disturb their pleasant monopoly, and weaken their control over the fisheries. A governor might take the part of the settlers; and they stoutly resisted his appointment. What they wanted was, as one of their own party expressed it, " that Newfoundland should always be considered as a great English ship, moored near the Banks, during the fishing season, for the convenience of English fishermen."

11. During this hard struggle the lot of these poor fishermen must have been very bitter. It is not wonderful to find that numbers of them, utterly disheartened, escaped to America, and there aided materially in building up the New England fisheries. In their little wooden hamlets, sprinkled along the sea-margin, their outlook was dreary enough. They had but a bare subsistence. They had no schools for their children, and no ministers of religion among them. All around were the dense woods, extending to the sea-shore, with a few paths cut through them. Before them was the great ocean, from which alone they were permitted to draw their means of subsistence. Their treatment was so harsh that if, in these days, the inmates of a prison or a workhouse were to be treated in like fashion, the public

would raise a shout of indignation. How could they advance in any of the arts of civilized life? They still held on, however; and, conscious that they had right on their side, they courageously resisted their selfish oppressors. The day of deliverance at last dawned. The British government at length found out that they had been misled and deceived by the representations of interested, selfish men, both in regard to the country and its fisheries. Restrictions on the settlement of the island were slowly removed one after another. The obnoxious statute of William III. was, however, left unrepealed, and greatly hindered improvements. It was not till less than eighty years ago that the last of these unjust laws was repealed, and people were allowed to possess land and build houses, and take some steps towards self-government.

12. The change for the better was brought about by the commodores and captains of the royal ships, which were periodically appointed to this station. They saw the terrible injustice which was inflicted on a patient, inoffensive people. One of them, named Lord Vere Beauclerk, a clear-headed, benevolent nobleman, made such strong representations to the Board of Trade that they appointed Capt. Henry Osborne to be the first governor of Newfoundland. The merchants protested against the appointment, but in vain. The new governor arrived in 1729.

13. A new era now began. Newfoundland, for the first time, was recognized as a British Colony. Though the Fishing Admirals were not abolished till long afterwards, they were now under control, and their power was more limited. The sufferings of the people were not ended, but they were diminished. The naval government of the island, under admirals and captains of

the British navy, now began, and was continued for many years. It was far from being the most desirable way of governing a colony; but it was a great improvement on anything yet enjoyed. The new system at least prepared the way for a local civil government, and finally for political freedom. In 1729, when the first governor arrived, the resident population had grown to be six thousand strong.

14. Whatever may have been the wrongs inflicted on the early settlers, we should clearly understand that no man or body of men, now living, should be held accountable for what was done in those distant days. The injustice of former ages has happily been rectified. The merchants and capitalists of to-day are men of a very different spirit and are in a very different position from those who once carried on the fisheries from England. They have no connection with old oppressions. Between them and the people of to-day the relations are cordial and friendly. Both can now unite for the advancement of their common country. Resentments and animosities between the two classes are, happily, things of the past.

QUESTIONS FOR EXAMINATION ON CHAPTER IX.

1. Give the population of Newfoundland in 1654; 1680; 1698. Did many come from England annually?

2. How did English merchants carry on the fishery? Why did they oppose the settlement of the island? In what state did they wish it kept?

3. How did the merchants persuade the English government to prevent people from settling?

4. What did the unjust laws forbid in order to prevent settlement? How long did these laws continue in force?

5. Did any persons make homes for themselves? What shows their vigour of character? What hardships had they to

endure? What order was issued in 1670? By whom? Who was to carry it out?

6. What prevented its full operation? How long was it till its revocation? What advantage did the merchants gain? What compromise was allowed? What proposal about women was afterwards issued?

7. Mention one of the laws about criminals in the reign of Charles I. How did the authority of the Fishing Admirals arise?

8. What did the Act of William III. establish? Why was the arrangement unjust?

9. How did the Fishing Admirals behave? What was their character?

10. Describe the sufferings of the resident population. What did they ask for? Why did the merchants oppose a governor? What use did they want to make of the island?

11. What was the condition of the settlers? What did the British government at length discover? What was done?

12. How did the change for the better come about? Who was the first governor, and what the date of his appointment?

13. Were the Fishing Admirals abolished? What was the benefit of the new government?

14. Is any one now living to be held accountable for the wrongs of the past?

MAP QUESTIONS. — CHAPTERS VIII. AND IX.

Where is Placentia? Bay of Bulls? Carbonear? Bonavista? Describe the position of Ryswick. (See note, Chapter VIII.)

NOTES AND EXPLANATIONS. — CHAPTER IX.

Lords of Trade and Plantations. — This Board was created to take charge of the colonies in America, but was of no service to them. In one of his speeches in the House of Commons, Burke said of it: "This Board is a sort of temperate bed of influence, — a sort of gently-ripening hot-house, — where eight members of Parliament receive salaries of a thousand a year for a given time, in order to mature, at a proper season, a claim to two thousand, granted for doing less, and on the credit of having toiled so long in the inferior laborious department." " It is a Board which, if *not mischievous, is of no use at all*."

This Board issued the inhuman order to Sir John Berry to burn the houses of the residents in Newfoundland and drive out the settlers. In 1676, six years after, John Downing, a resident, by his strong appeals, succeeded in procuring an order from the king to annul it. Sir Joshua Childs, the principal merchant connected with the fisheries in England, was the means of procuring this barbarous edict from the Lords of Trade. He must have realized much wealth from the fisheries, for, when his daughter married the eldest son of the Duke of Beaufort, he gave her a portion of £50,000. He had fish-ponds in Epping Forest, " many miles in circuit." He was also engaged in the East India trade.

CHRONOLOGICAL SUMMARY. — FROM 1600 TO 1700.

A.D.
1593. Richard Apsham's expedition to Newfoundland.
1603. James I., King of England.
1607. Jamestown founded in Virginia.
1608. Quebec founded by Champlain.
1609. Hudson River discovered by Henry Hudson.
1610. Guy's settlement in Conception Bay.
1613. First child of European parents born in Newfoundland.
1615. Whitbourne's commission to Newfoundland.
1618. Sir Walter Raleigh beheaded.
1620. Landing of the Pilgrim Fathers in New England.
1623. Sir George Calvert's patent for colonization of Newfoundland.
1625. Charles I., King of England.
1630. Arrival of first Irish settlers in Newfoundland.
1636. Rhode Island Colony founded.
1638. Sir David Kirk's patent in Newfoundland.
Connecticut founded.
1641. Montreal founded by the Jesuit Fathers.
1642. Civil War in England between Charles I. and the Parliament.
1643. Louis XIV., King of France.
Union of the New England Colonies.
1645. Battle of Naseby. — Close of the Civil War.
1649. Execution of Charles I.

1658. Death of Cromwell.
1660. Placentia founded by the French.
Charles II., King of England.
1665. Great Plague of London.
1670. Sir John Berry ordered to destroy settlements in Newfoundland.
1673. Marquette and Joliet's discovery of the Mississippi.
1679. Habeas-corpus Act.
1685. James II., King of England.
1688. English Revolution, — Expulsion of the Stuarts.
1689. William III. and Mary, Sovereigns of England.
1696. Nesmond's Repulse at St. John's, Newfoundland.
First capture of St. John's by the French.
1697. Treaty of Ryswick.

EMINENT PERSONS FROM 1600 TO 1700.

Ben Jonson; Massinger; Jeremy Taylor; Milton; Locke; Molière; Kepler; Sir Isaac Newton; Turenne; Bayle; Dryden; Bunyan; Reubens; Vandyke; Inigo Jones; Sir Christopher Wren.

CHAPTER X.

FROM 1697 TO 1754.

RENEWED EFFORTS OF THE FRENCH TO CONQUER NEWFOUNDLAND.

TREATY OF UTRECHT. — DISPUTES CONNECTED WITH IT. — CONFLICT BETWEEN THE GOVERNORS AND FISHING ADMIRALS. — COMMISSION OF OYER AND TERMINER.

1. We must now take up the history of the island from the treaty of Ryswick, in 1697. The thirty years which followed constituted the darkest and dreariest period in the experience of the oppressed settlers. Their difficulties and sufferings were such that it seems marvellous that they were not driven to settle in some more favorable region, and to abandon in despair the effort to make homes for themselves in Newfoundland.

2. The peace between England and France, secured by the treaty of Ryswick, was of short duration. In 1702, in the commencement of Queen Anne's reign, war recommenced. The French were strongly established in Placentia and other places along the southern shore. From these centres they carried on their fisheries round the island, and greatly interfered with the English and resident fishermen. Captain Leake, a distinguished naval officer, was sent to check their encroachments. He destroyed several of their settlements on the southern shore, and dismantled their fortifications at the Island of St. Pierre; but he left them still in possession of their chief stronghold, Placentia. An unsuccessful attempt was made to reduce this place in the following

year. Then the French became bolder and more confident, and at length determined to seize the whole island. They attacked St. John's, but were there repulsed. Then they assailed the smaller settlements, burning and destroying, inflicting great miseries on the people and carrying off a number of them as prisoners. Under the protection of their war-vessels, they carried on their fisheries in the northern harbours. A force was organized in St. John's which made a successful raid upon these French war-ships and captured six out of ten of them. Two years after, in 1708, the French, in the middle of winter, despatched a force from Placentia, which landed within fifteen miles of St. John's, marched overland, surprised the unprepared garrison, and captured the place. Then they assailed Carbonear; but once more, the brave defenders beat off the French. Newfoundland was now, for a time, lost to the British empire.

3. But if the arms of France were successful in these petty conflicts they sustained terrible reverses on the continent of Europe. In four great battles, the famous English commander, the Duke of Marlborough, so shattered the military power of France, that Louis XIV. was glad to accept terms of peace on terms very disadvantageous to himself. This war was brought to a close by the celebrated treaty of Utrecht (pronounced *O-o-trekt*), which marks a very important era in the history of Newfoundland. By the provisions of this treaty the French agreed to surrender all their possessions in Newfoundland and the adjacent islands, and to retire from Placentia. Thus the sovereignty of the whole island was secured to England.

4. But, though the French had no longer any territorial rights, unfortunately for the peace and prosperity

of the colony this treaty gave them the right of fishing and curing fish on the western and northern shores of the island. Thus the people were doomed still to be hindered in their industrial labours by the presence of the French, when it would have been an easy matter, in drawing up the treaty, to get rid of them entirely, and make the island truly an undivided possession of England. The privilege thus given to the French has led to disputes, which are not settled to this day. The French have ever since tried to maintain that the treaty gave them the *sole right* of fishing along a certain part of the coast, and therefore that Newfoundland fishermen had no right to fish in these waters. On the other hand, Newfoundland denies that any such *exclusive right* was given by the treaty, and holds that her people have a right to fish concurrently, or side by side with the French, so long as they do not interrupt their fishing operations.

5. England has never admitted the exclusive right of the French to these fisheries. In order, however, to preserve peace, she has discouraged Newfoundland fishermen from going on this portion of the coast, leaving the whole question unsettled from generation to generation. The consequences have been most injurious to Newfoundland. Her people have been virtually excluded from the best portion of the island, which has been left in a wilderness state; and they could neither prosecute the fisheries there, nor settle the lands, or carry on mining or other industries.

6. In spite of all these difficulties people began to settle on that portion of the coast where the French had these fishing-privileges. They continued to increase, year after year, and at length numbered nearly nine thousand persons. They were without laws or magistrates; without roads, schools, or any civilizing influences. At last the condition of these outlaws could no longer be overlooked. The British government, only so lately as 1878, permitted magistrates to be appointed, and custom-houses built. Four years later they allowed the local government to issue grants of land and licenses for mining. They also permitted the people to elect two representatives to the House of Assembly. Thus the shadowy claims of the French to control the land were forever set aside. This was a most important step, as it incorporated this region with the rest of the island, and placed it under the jurisdiction of the local government, giving the people the rights of citizens. The only question now awaiting settlement has reference to the "exclusive" and "concurrent" right. There is reason to hope that this too will be satisfactorily arranged. Then "the French Shore Question," as it is called, will be finally disposed of.

7. We saw, at the close of last chapter, how the British government, in 1729, at length appointed a governor of the island in the person of Captain Henry Osborne. This step greatly alarmed the merchants, lest it might interfere with their profitable and uncontrolled dominion over the people and the fisheries. Accordingly, they set themselves vigorously to work to counteract the measure, and to prevent any lawful authority from taking root in the country. They continued to support the tyrannical jurisdiction of the detested Fishing Admirals, and refused to recognize the newly appointed authority.

8. Captain Osborne, on his arrival, proceeded to divide the island into districts, and appoint justices of the peace, selected from the best classes of the people, with constables under them. The Fishing Admirals

fiercely opposed the exercise of authority by these justices, and declared their appointment was illegal. They told the people the justices were usurpers, and endeavoured to bring them into contempt.

9. Unfortunately, the new system had been introduced by "an order in Council," whereas the Fishing Admirals claimed that they had been appointed by an Act of Parliament, and, therefore, had superior authority. The conflict between the two went on for nearly fifty years, the governors sustaining the justices, and the West Country merchants backing the Fishing Admirals. The good effects of the appointment of a governor were thus greatly impeded. Besides, he only resided in the colony about three or four months in each year, returning to England in October. It was not till 1818 that a resident governor was appointed.

10. Thus, for another half century the people had to suffer under cruel misrule. It was then, indeed, no longer illegal to settle in the country; but still no permission was yet given to cultivate the soil, and no stage could be erected for handling fish by the residents till their lords and masters from England had been accommodated. Besides, the fishermen were so poor that they had to obtain advances in provisions and clothing, at very high prices, at the beginning of each fishing-season, and at the close to pay for them in fish, the price of which was fixed by the supplier. Thus arose the "supplying system," which kept the fishermen constantly in debt and dependence. The adherents of the old system never ceased their attacks on the new, and were constantly petitioning the home authorities to have it altered or extinguished. But the British government were firm in their refusal to withdraw the small measure of civil government granted to the colony. The right

prevailed. Slowly, and step by step, improvements came. The resident population increased in numbers and influence. The Fishing Admirals and their supporters saw it was useless to continue the conflict, and at length they and their claims to authority fell into well-merited contempt, and passed into oblivion.

11. The year 1750 witnessed another important step in the extension of civil government in the Island. Hitherto all criminals had to be sent to England for trial. Witnesses had also to proceed there, at great expense and inconvenience. Justice was often defeated, and great hardships endured. Successive governors had pointed out this evil. At length, in 1750, Captain Drake, the governor, was authorized to establish a court in which all criminal cases could be tried within the bounds of the colony. Those who presided in this court were called "Commissioners of Oyer and Terminer."

12. In 1754 the representative of the Baltimore family presented a claim to be put in possession of the province of Avalon, on the strength of the original grant of 1623, to the first Lord Baltimore. The application was rejected by the law officers of the Crown, on the ground that the Baltimore family had not held possession for 130 years, and that later grants had set their claim aside. No more was heard of the matter.

QUESTIONS FOR EXAMINATION ON CHAPTER X.

1. What was the condition of the resident people for thirty years after the treaty of Ryswick?

2. When did war recommence? Where were the French established in the island? Who was sent to remove them, and what did he do? Describe the movements of the French. What did war-ships from St. John's accomplish at the North? When

was St. John's taken the second time by the French, and how? What of Carbonear?

3. What led to the treaty of Utrecht? What were its provisions as regards Newfoundland?

4. What fishing privileges did the French acquire by the treaty of Utrecht? What have been the injurious effects of giving the French such privileges? What do the French claim by this treaty? What is the view of Newfoundland on this point?

5. What has England done in connection with these privileges? What injury has the colony suffered?

6. In what state were people living on the so-called "French Shore"? When were magistrates first appointed there? When were the people there allowed to send representatives? When were land grants allowed? What important change is thus made?

7. Who supported the Fishing Admirals against the governors?

8. What improvements did Captain Osborne effect?

9. What advantage had the Fishing Admirals in the contest? How long did it last? Did governors live in the island? When was the first resident governor appointed?

10. Describe the condition of the people at this time. How did the "supplying system" arise? What were its effects? What was the end of the Fishing Admirals?

11. What great improvement came in 1750?

12. What claim did the Baltimore family make? Why was it refused?

MAP QUESTIONS.

Describe the position of the island of St. Pierre. Of Utrecht (see note). On what part of the coast have the French fishing-privileges in Newfoundland?

NOTES AND EXPLANATIONS.—CHAPTER X.

French Claims.—Lord Palmerston's note to Count Sebastiani, the French ambassador, in 1838, on the subject of the French claims to an exclusive fishing right in Newfoundland, may be regarded as conclusive. In it he says: "The British Government has never understood the declaration to have had for its object to deprive the British subjects of the right to participate with the French in taking fish at sea off that coast, provided they did so without interrupting the French cod-fishery."

He further states that in no public document or Act of Parliament "does it appear that the right of French subjects to an exclusive fishery, either of codfish or fish generally, is specifically recognized."

Utrecht is the capital of the Dutch province of that name, which lies between Holland, Gelderland, and the Zuyder-Zee. The city is divided into two parts by the Rhine. At the British minister's house in Utrecht, in 1713, was signed the treaty which ended " the War of the Spanish Succession," or, as it is called in America, " Queen Anne's War." The Duke of Marlborough's great victories were Blenheim (1704) ; Ramilies (1706) ; Oudenarde (1798) ; Malplaquet (1709).

CHRONOLOGICAL SUMMARY, 1700 TO 1760.

A.D.
1702. Anne Queen of England.
1704. Gibraltar taken by the English.
Battle of Blenheim.
1707. Union of English and Scottish Parliaments.
1708. Second Capture of St. John's by the French.
1713. Treaty of Utrecht.
1714. George I.. King of England.
1715. Louis XV., King of France.
1725. Death of Peter the Great.
1727. George II., King of England.
1729. Captain Henry Osborne first governor of Newfoundland.
1733. Colony of Georgia founded.
1745. Louisburg taken by the English under Pepperel and Warren.
1748. Peace of Aix-la-Chapelle ; Louisburg restored to the French.
1750. Court of Oyer and Terminer established in Newfoundland.
1759. Quebec taken by Wolfe.
1760. George III., King of England.

EMINENT PERSONS, FROM 1700 TO 1760.

Sir Robert Walpole ; William Pitt ; Swift ; Pope ; Hume ; Defoe ; Gibbon ; Voltaire ; Rousseau ; Montesquieu ; Franklin ; Maria Theresa Wesley ; Whitfield ; Johnson ; Goldsmith ; Franklin ; Wolfe.

CHAPTER XI.

FROM 1756 TO 1775.

"THE SEVEN YEARS' WAR."

CAPITULATION OF LOUISBURG AND QUEBEC. — CAPTURE OF ST. JOHN'S BY THE FRENCH. — THEIR EXPULSION. — TREATY OF PARIS. — LABRADOR ADDED TO NEWFOUNDLAND. — INTRODUCTION OF CUSTOMS AND THE NAVIGATION LAWS. — RELIGIOUS INTOLERANCE IN NEWFOUNDLAND.

1. THE final struggle between England and France for the control of North America commenced in 1756. The contest is known as "The Seven Years' War." Warlike operations on both sides began on sea and land; but the chief battle-ground was America. William Pitt, " the Great Commoner," as he was called, assumed the guidance of affairs, as Prime Minister of England. He began the campaign by an expedition against Louisburg, in Cape Breton, a strong fortress held by France. The military command of this expedition was given to Colonel Jeffrey Amherst, Colonel James Wolfe being second in command, and Admiral Boscawen commander of the fleet. Louisburg was captured, and two years afterwards the fortifications of that formidable fortress were razed to the ground. The crowning expedition, in 1759, was directed against Quebec. Wolfe, who had greatly distinguished himself for bravery and skill at the siege of Louisburg, was placed in supreme command. Quebec fell, and Wolfe " died happy," in the moment of victory, on the Plains of Abraham. The power of France in the New World was completely broken.

The whole of North America passed into the possession of the British crown.

2. Though the French had now lost the magnificent colony of Canada, they still clung most tenaciously to the idea of conquering and holding Newfoundland. They knew its value, in connection with the prosecution of their fisheries, which they still looked to as the great training-school for their seamen. Accordingly, in 1762, they resolved on another expedition for the conquest of the island. A strong naval squadron was collected at Brest, and on the 24th of June, it arrived at the Bay of Bulls. Here a force was landed, which marched overland, and surprised and overpowered the small garrison at St. John's, consisting of but sixty-three men. The French then proceeded to strengthen the fortifications. Their fleet anchored in the harbour. They succeeded, soon after, in capturing Carbonear and Trinity, and devastated the trade and fisheries, inflicting great sufferings on the people.

Captain Graves, the Governor, was then on his way out from England to the island. On the Banks he was met by a sloop which informed him of the capture of St. John's. By this vessel he immediately sent despatches to Lord Colville, commander at Halifax, who at once sailed with a strong naval force, and blockaded the harbour of St. John's, where the French fleet lay.

3. Meantime Governor Graves landed at Placentia, and proceeded to put the fortifications, which were in a ruinous state, in a proper condition of defence. Lord Colville was speedily joined by Colonel Amherst, with 800 Highlanders, from Louisburg. These troops were landed at Torbay, six miles north of St. John's, under a heavy fire from the French. They advanced on the capital, over hills and very difficult ground, suffering

from a continual bush-fire from the French, who had taken to the woods. The gallant Highlanders then rushed on the strong post of Quidi Vidi, which they carried, sword in hand. Signal Hill, a lofty eminence overlooking the harbour, was held by the French, in considerable force. Led by Captain Macdonald, the Highlanders charged up the rugged heights, in the face of a heavy fire from the enemy; and the hill was taken by storm. The brave leader and his lieutenant both fell mortally wounded. Four men were killed, in the final assault, and eighteen wounded. In all, the English lost twenty men.

4. The French fleet were now shut in the harbour by Colville's blockading squadron, and their surrender seemed inevitable. But, at this critical time, a storm arose, which drove off the English ships. Taking advantage of this, and favoured by a fog, the French fleet put to sea, and escaped. The garrison, after a brief struggle, surrendered, on condition that the troops should be conveyed to France. Thus ended the last serious attempt on the part of the French to gain possession of Newfoundland.

5. The year in which the French were thus both triumphant and defeated at St. John's witnessed the close of " the Seven Years' War," by the treaty of Paris, in 1763. By this treaty England gained a totality of empire in North America, extending from Hudson's Bay to the mouth of the Mississippi. France renounced all claims to Canada, Acadia, Cape Breton, and Newfoundland. Unfortunately, however, this treaty confirmed and extended the French fishing privileges in Newfoundland, which had been secured by the treaty of Utrecht. The islands of St. Pierre and Miquelon, at the mouth of Fortune Bay, were transferred to France, as a shelter for her fishermen, on condition that no fortifications were to be erected, and that only a guard of fifty men, for police purposes, should be maintained there. This grant greatly strengthened the hold of the French on the island, in connection with their fisheries, and led to perpetual jealousies and discords, greatly retarding the progress of the country.

6. In order to establish at Labrador a free fishery, open to all British subjects, the whole of its extensive coast was placed under the care of the Governor of Newfoundland, whose title, henceforth, was to be " Governor and Commander-in-chief in and over the island of Newfoundland, and of all the coast of Labrador, from the entrance of Hudson's Bay to the river of St. John's, opposite the island of Anticosti." This addition conferred increased importance on the government of the colony, and led its people, in after years, to prosecute the valuable fisheries at Labrador, where, at the present time, one-third of all the codfish exported is taken.

7. Another important step in advance was taken in 1764. On the representation of the Board of Trade a collector and controller of customs for Newfoundland was appointed, and the navigation laws were extended to the island, which was now formally declared to be " one of His Majesty's Plantations " or colonies. This was a fatal blow to the old system, by which it was kept merely as a fishing-station for the benefit of a few monopolists.

8. A census was taken, at the close of 1763, from which it appeared that the population of the island numbered 13,112. Of these, 7,500 were constant residents in the island, of whom 4,795 were Roman Catholics, and 2,705 were Protestants. The cod-fishery was in a thriving condition, 386,274 quintals of cod having been made

that year, of which two-thirds were caught and cured by the resident portion of the population, who were gradually getting the upper hand in carrying on the fisheries. Besides, 694 tierces of salmon and 1,598 tons of oil were exported; and 371 vessels carried on the trade with the mother-country and the New England colonies. The intercourse with Ireland was, at this time, considerable. Numbers of Irish emigrants came out as settlers, and large quantities of fish were sent to Cork, Waterford, and Belfast, the vessels bringing return cargoes of provisions. In 1765 the export of cod was 493,654 quintals, being an increase of 145,360 quintals in two years. There was, of course, a corresponding increase in the wealth and general comforts of the people.

9. But, though improvements were thus slowly making way, the social condition of the people was still deplorable. The administration of justice, especially in the outlying settlements, was very defective. The magistrates were often ignorant, incompetent men, who were grossly partial in their decisions, and at times open to bribery. The high charges by employers for advances in food and clothing, at the commencement of the fishing season, often left little at the close to enable the poor fishermen to provide necessaries during the long winter. Too often the fishermen found themselves in debt when the season's work was over. Tempted by want, some of these were guilty of acts of violence or theft; others fled to New England to escape the miseries of their condition. As yet no one could own any portion of the land for purposes of cultivation; and if any one enclosed a plot of ground it was lawful for any other who chose to take down such fences and enclosures. The stormy ocean alone was free to the people; and on its uncertain harvests they had to subsist. The wealth won by their

toil did not remain in the island, but went to enrich other countries. We must admire the spirit and energy of a people who, amid these hardships and tyrannies, continued to cling to the soil, and bravely pioneered the way for happier generations.

10. But at this time another bitter and shameful ingredient was added to their social oppressions. Religious intolerance and persecution broke out, and for over thirty years continued to exert a baneful influence on society, and to sow the seeds of bitterness and strife. The objects of this intolerance were the adherents of the Roman Catholic faith, and those who subjected them to persecution were the ruling authorities of the colony, who then wielded despotic power. We, who live in happier and more enlightened days, now look back with sorrow and shame upon these deeds of intolerance which we see to have been wrong and unjust. The intercourse with Ireland had led to the settlement in Newfoundland of numbers of Irish, and these were constantly increasing. Some of them had fled from the oppression of penal laws in their own land; but the exiles met the same spirit of intolerance in this distant colony. The successive governors appear to have regarded these Irish emigrants with dislike and distrust; and, in order to discourage their coming, and to lessen their numbers, laws were enacted to prevent them from enjoying the exercise of their religious worship. Priests could only enter the country in disguise; and, if discovered when engaged in the administration of the rites of their religion, were liable to be arrested. Masters of ships were ordered to carry back such Irish passengers as they brought out, at the close of each fishing season. These harsh and unjust regulations continued to be enforced by successive governors. As usual, persecution failed to accomplish its object. Emigrants continued to arrive from Ireland in spite of the disabilities under which the adherents of Catholicism laboured. Their clergy followed them in disguise, and secretly ministered to their flocks. At length a better spirit prevailed. In 1784 a royal proclamation ended forever religious persecution. Liberty of conscience was granted, and the free exercise of their modes of worship was secured to Roman Catholics.

11. In judging of these errors of the past let us remember that the principles of religious freedom are of very slow growth, and even yet are far from being fully recognized in many Christian countries. When these persecutions were going on in Newfoundland the spirit of intolerance was strong in England, and religious freedom was neither understood nor practised. The very men who were most conscientious in maintaining their own religious views were often the most zealous in putting down all who differed from them. Very few had yet learned to acknowledge the great principle that men have a right to worship God according to the way they believe to be best. Some claimed toleration for themselves, but were unable to discover that people who differed from them were as truly entitled to be tolerated as they themselves were.

12. Our condemnation of these acts of intolerance in the past should be mingled with pity for those who were so blinded as to be guilty of them. Those who now enjoy a clearer light should never lose sight of the great truth that men should be free to hold their own religious views, and to worship in the way which their consciences approve. If this be acted on, harmony, kindness, and mutual good-will among all classes of worshippers will prevail, and sectarian strifes and persecutions will be unknown.

QUESTIONS FOR EXAMINATION ON CHAPTER XI.

1. When did the Seven Years' War begin? Where was the chief battle-ground? Who was then Prime Minister in England? When was Louisburg taken? Who captured Quebec? What was the result?

2. Describe the capture of St. John's by the French, in 1762. Where was the Governor at the time?

3. Describe the recapture of St. John's by the English.

4. How did the French fleet escape?

5. Give the date of the Treaty of Paris. How did this treaty affect the Newfoundland fisheries?

6. What addition to the jurisdiction of Newfoundland was made in 1763? What was the effect?

7. What change occurred in 1764, and what effect had it?

8. What was the population in 1763? Give the exports of that year, and of 1765.

9. What was the condition of the people at this time? Mention their disadvantages.

10. What form did religious persecution take, and who suffered by it? Who inflicted it? When did it cease?

11. What led to this religious intolerance? What is the meaning of religious freedom?

12. How is good-will to be maintained among those who differ in religion?

MAP QUESTIONS.

Describe the situation of Louisburg and Quebec. Point out Labrador, and give its dimensions. (See note.) Where are Bay of Bulls? Trinity? Carbonear? Cork? Waterford? Belfast?

NOTES AND EXPLANATIONS. — CHAPTER XI.

William Pitt. — Born in 1708, died 1778. He was one of the most eminent of English statesmen. He was noted for his brilliant powers of debate, his eloquence, and the keenness of his sarcasm. He entered Parliament before he was twenty-one years of age, and took the lead against Sir Robert Walpole. He owes his chief fame as a minister to his conduct of the war in which he found his country involved when he was called to the head of affairs. In 1766 he retired from the House of Commons, — the scene of his glory, — and went to the House of Lords as Earl of Chatham. He was buried in Westminster Abbey, and a monument was erected to his memory at the public expense. His distinguished son, the Right Honourable William Pitt, became Prime Minister in 1783, when but twenty-four years of age; a post which he held for seventeen years, during a most momentous period in the history of England. He died, in 1806, at the age of forty-seven.

General Wolfe. — Born at Westerham, in Kent, in 1727. He distinguished himself in continental wars. The discerning eye of Pitt selected him for the great enterprise against Quebec. On the night of September 12, 1759, Wolfe, with a detachment of his troops, embarked in boats on the St. Lawrence, bound on the desperate enterprise of scaling the Heights of Abraham. The night was clear and calm. Wolfe was in the foremost boat, and as the flotilla dropped down with the tide, his low voice was heard repeating to his officers the stanzas of " Grey's Elegy in a Country Churchyard," which had recently appeared. It may be that a presentiment of his own approaching death gave a mournful pathos to his voice as he uttered the touching words, " The paths of glory lead but to the grave." When he had finished, he added, "Now, gentlemen, I would rather have written those lines than take Quebec to-morrow." When the sun rose next morning the French saw with astonishment the Plains of Abraham glittering with arms, and the British gathered in battle array. The gallant Montcalm marched out to meet his foe. Wolfe, in leading on his soldiers, fell mortally wounded. Ere he breathed his last, one of his officers exclaimed, " See, they run!" — "Who run?" asked Wolfe. — " The enemy; they give way everywhere." — "Now God be praised," said the hero; "I die happy." Montcalm was also fatally wounded. Being told he could not live long, he replied, " So much the better. I shall not live to see the surrender of Quebec."

" The victory on the Plains of Abraham and the downfall of Quebec," says Parkman, "filled all England with pride and exultation. From north to south the land blazed with illuminations, and resounded with the ringing of bells, the firing of guns, and the shouts of the multitude. In one village alone all was dark and silent amid the general joy, for there dwelt the mother of Wolfe. The populace, with unwonted delicacy, respected her lonely sorrow, and forbore to obtrude the sound of their rejoicings upon the grief for one who had been through life her pride and solace, and had repaid her love with a tender and constant devotion."

Wolfe fell at the early age of thirty-four. His remains were brought to England, and interred at Greenwich. Parliament voted him a monument in Westminster Abbey.

French Capture of St. John's, 1762. — Anspach, in his "History of Newfoundland," makes honourable mention of two merchants whose public services were essentially useful at this critical time, when the French took St. John's. One of these was Robert Carter, a merchant at Ferryland, who, by his prudence and indefatigable exertions, found means to procure a sufficient supply of provisions and other necessaries, for the support not only of the garrison at the Isle of Boys, but also of a considerable number of distressed inhabitants, who had retired thither for protection and relief, from the 24th of June to the 9th of October. The other was Charles Garland, then a merchant and justice of the peace in the district of Conception Bay. Carbonear Island was then deemed a place where a battery could be useful to the port and to the neighbouring settlements. Mr. Garland supplied, at his own expense, and for a considerable time, a small detachment which he had obtained from head-quarters for that small island, with firewood, provisions, and additional pay, until the French took it and destroyed the works and batteries. Mr. Garland also procured a number of seamen for the English squadron. His services were honourably acknowledged by the government, and he was indemnified for his expenses.

On board Lord Colville's flag-ship, the "Northumberland," when it came to the relief of St. John's, was Captain Cook, afterwards celebrated for his voyages round the world. He then held the position of "master" on board the flag-ship, having entered the navy as a common sailor. Governor Graves had formed a high opinion of Cook, and secured for him the conduct of a naval survey of Newfoundland, on which he spent three years. His charts of the coasts of Newfoundland and Labrador are found wonderfully accurate, even when the work is done over again, with the improved instruments of the present day. In this arduous service Cook won his first laurels, and proved himself an able mathematician. Sir Hugh Palliser, the Governor, had a warm esteem for him. After most distinguished services in exploring the Southern ocean, and charting the Australian coast, he engaged in an Arctic expedition. In 1779 he was killed in an accidental quarrel with the natives of Owhyhee, one of the Sandwich Islands.

Labrador.—The great peninsula of Labrador is 1,100 miles in length, and 600 miles in breadth, its area being 420,000 square miles. Only the eastern portion is under the jurisdiction of Newfoundland, the rest being annexed to the Dominion of Canada. The boundary between the two is a line drawn due north and south from Blanc Sablon to Cape Chudleigh. Such is the extraordinary fish-wealth of Labrador, that between 20,000 and 25,000 fishermen visit its shores during the summer months. Its fisheries are now mainly carried on by Newfoundland fishermen. In 1881, over 400,000 quintals of codfish were taken on Labrador, besides herrings and salmon.

The Esquimaux of Labrador, among whom Moravian missionaries have long laboured with success, number 1,700; the Indians of the interior 4,000; the resident white population on the eastern coast, 2,400. On the St. Lawrence coast there is a population of 4,400; making a total of 12,500. The climate is very severe, and the country is unfit to be a residence of civilized man.

CHAPTER XII.

FROM 1775 TO 1814.

PALLISER'S ACT.

AMERICAN REVOLUTION. — RELIGIOUS FREEDOM ESTABLISHED IN NEWFOUNDLAND. — TREATY OF VERSAILLES. — SUPREME COURT ESTABLISHED. — WAR WITH FRANCE. — GREAT PROSPERITY OF THE FISHERIES. — LAND RESTRICTIONS LESSENED. — MUTINY DETECTED IN THE GARRISON AT ST. JOHN'S. — VARIOUS IMPROVEMENTS.

1. The infant settlements in Newfoundland, now growing into strength and importance, received some recognition and encouragement in 1775. The British Parliament passed an act which was known in the island as "Palliser's Act," as it was drawn up at the recommendation of Captain Palliser, who had recently held the office of Governor. This act still kept alive the principle of a ship-fishery carried on from England, but introduced some useful regulations. Among other things it directed all agreements between masters and servants to be made in writing, and that no more than one-half of the wages of the latter should at any time be advanced to them. It also declared that all fish and oil taken and made by the employer should be liable, in the first place, for the payment of the servants' wages. This last provision was especially beneficial, as it secured the payment of the hardly-earned wages of the fishermen at the close of the season, and ended the disputes long prevalent between masters and servants on this subject. To insure the return of the fishermen to Eng-

land, this act authorized the masters to detain forty shillings out of their wages for paying their passages home. By the same act a bounty was given to vessels engaged in the Bank fishery.

2. But now a new source of trouble presented itself, which entailed severe sufferings and losses on the whole population. A war arose between Great Britain and her revolted colonies in North America, in 1775. It did not terminate till 1782, when England acknowledged the independence of the United States. The first Congress of the revolted colonies passed a decree forbidding all exports to British possessions. This blow fell with special severity upon the inhabitants of Newfoundland, who, for a lengthened period, had been accustomed to obtain their supplies of food from the New England States. The annual import of such produce amounted, at that time, to £345,000 per annum. Gloom and despondency prevailed throughout the island, owing to the apprehended scarcity of provisions. The difficulty was met by detaching vessels from the fishery and sending them to Ireland for supplies of food. American privateers appeared on the coast, and, entering some of the harbours, destroyed much valuable property. British cruisers, however, were sent, which speedily drove off the privateers, capturing and burning a number of them. St. John's was at once put in a state of defence, and a new fort, called Fort Townsend, was erected to protect the harbour. A detachment of soldiers and a supply of arms arrived from England to aid the people in defending themselves. Ships of war were kept constantly cruising around the coast. France declared in favour of the United States, and war was commenced between France and England. Rear-Admiral Montague, who was then Governor of Newfoundland, captured the isl-

ands of St. Pierre and Miquelon, which had been ceded to France, and sent nearly two thousand of the French inhabitants home to their own country.

3. At length the unhappy war between England and her colonies ended, in 1782, in the recognition of the independence of the United States. This introduced an immediate change for the better in Newfoundland. Its trade and industries revived. The people were no longer harassed by the attacks of privateers and the dread of invasion. After a time commercial intercourse with the United States was resumed, and importations of food, but only in British ships at first, were permitted.

4. In 1782 Vice-Admiral John Campbell was appointed Governor of the island. The increasing importance of its trade and fisheries had led to the appointment of officers of a higher rank than that of captains and commodores to take charge of its government, the first of whom was Rear-Admiral Montague. Governor Campbell proved to be a man of an enlightened and liberal spirit. To him the people were indebted for terminating the reign of religious intolerance and persecution. He issued an order, in 1784, to all magistrates throughout the island, which ran as follows: "Pursuant to the King's instructions to me, you are to allow all persons inhabiting this island to have full liberty of conscience, and the free exercise of all such modes of religious worship as are not prohibited by law, provided they be content with a quiet and peaceable enjoyment of the same, not giving offence or scandal to government." The year which witnessed this happy change brought the Rev. Dr. O'Donnell, a Roman Catholic clergyman, to the island. He at once obtained full liberty to erect a place of worship, to celebrate mar-

riages, and to perform all the rites and ceremonies of his Church. He was the first authorized Roman Catholic missionary in the island after it became a purely British possession. In 1796 he was appointed Vicar-Apostolic and Bishop.

5. Clergymen of the Church of England had been labouring in the island from 1703; but it was not till 1787 that a Bishop was appointed from Nova Scotia, and Newfoundland was attached to his see. Wesleyan Methodism in the island dates from 1765, when a single minister, the Rev. Lawrence Coughlan, planted it; but it was not till 1786 that three missionaries arrived to follow up his labours. English dissent was represented as early as 1775 by a single Congregational Church in St. John's. Governor Campbell, in 1782, renewed permission for a continuation of its services. Thus, happily, all Christian denominations henceforth enjoyed equal freedom of worship.

6. The war between England and France was terminated by the Treaty of Versailles in 1783. This treaty altered the boundaries of that portion of the coast of Newfoundland on which the French had rights of fishing. It was agreed that henceforth the French fishing should commence at Cape St. John, situated on the eastern coast of the island, in about 50° of latitude, and going round to the north, and down the western coast, should have for boundary Cape Ray. This change was beneficial, as it defined accurately the boundaries, about which previously there had been many quarrels.

7. The year 1793 was marked by a beneficial change in the administration of justice, which may be truly said to have constituted a new era in Newfoundland. This was the establishment of a Supreme Court of Judicature, and the appointment of a Chief Justice. After

the authority of the " Fishing Admirals " had come to
an end the commanders of the King's ships, visiting
the island in summer, were commissioned by the Governor to administer justice. Under the title of "Surrogates," or deputies of the Governor, they held courts
in different places and determined causes. During their
absence, in winter, Courts of Session, composed of justices of the peace for the several districts, assumed the
administration of justice. The Court of Admiralty had
been unduly extending its powers, and frequently came
into collision with the other courts, thus causing great
confusion and dissatisfaction. The authority of all
these courts was brought to an end, in 1793, by the
creation of a Supreme Court for the whole island, having
full power to try all persons charged with crimes and
misdemeanours, and to determine all suits and complaints of a civil nature. Chief Justice Reeves was
the first president of the Supreme Court. He was a man
of high character and great legal ability. He published
a " History of the Government of Newfoundland," in
which he faithfully and fearlessly laid bare the causes of
the evils which afflicted the country. He showed conclusively that the merchant adventurers, for their own
selfish purposes, had been endeavouring to keep all
power in their own hands, so as to exclude competition
from without or within; and that their policy had prevented the settlement of the country and the proper
administration of justice. Among the benefactors of
Newfoundland, Chief Justice Reeves deserves to hold
a foremost place. He effected many beneficial changes
in the administration of justice; but such was the force
of old customs that it was not till 1824 that an act was
passed completely abolishing the old Surrogates and
Sessions Courts, and appointing two judges to assist the

Chief Justice. The whole island was then divided into three districts, in each of which a court was appointed to be held every year.

8. The French Revolution of 1789 must be regarded, in its far-reaching results, as one of the most stupendous events of modern times. The war between France and England, which broke out in 1793, had a most important influence on the fortunes of Newfoundland. It was anticipated that the French would again try to get possession of the island. Admiral Wallace, the Governor, called on the people to aid in protecting their homes against a French invasion. They responded to his call in a most loyal spirit. Volunteers flocked to the national standard, and a corps of six hundred men was formed in addition to the volunteer force. The forts were strengthened, and new batteries made ready for action. In 1796 a French squadron appeared off the harbour of St. John's; but, finding that a hot reception was prepared for them, they passed on without challenging a shot. They succeeded in burning the defenceless settlement of Bay of Bulls, and, after this small exploit, disappeared. No hostile force has, since that exciting day, fired the warlike ardour of the inhabitants, or threatened the peace of the rising settlements.

9. The gigantic struggle between England and France, which did not end till 1814, gave a remarkable impulse to the prosperity of the colony. England was mistress of the seas; the French could no longer prosecute the fisheries on the Banks or around the shores of the island. The supply of the fish-markets of Europe fell exclusively into the hands of the Newfoundland merchants. Fish rose to an unprecedented price. In 1799, 400 vessels were engaged in the trade of the country, and about 2,000 boats. The export of fish reached

500,000 quintals. The capital invested in the fisheries of cod, salmon, and seals was not less than £1,500,000 sterling. The seal-fishery, which had before been prosecuted only on a small scale, now attained large dimensions, and brought in much wealth. In 1804 the number of seals taken was 106,739. Population rapidly increased. In 1804 the resident population was 20,380; while the fishermen who returned to England at the close of the season numbered over 4,000. In 1807 the population of St. John's had risen to 5,000, and in 1812 to 7,075. The war between England and the United States, which began in 1812, removed the competition of American fishermen, and a complete monopoly of European fish-markets followed. Fish rose to three times its usual price, reaching, at length, forty-five shillings sterling per quintal. The fisheries, too, were abundant during several years. The wages of the fishermen increased in proportion. Large numbers of emigrants arrived from Ireland. In 1814, 7,000 came, and the following year 4,000 more. From 1812 to 1816 the population of St. John's nearly doubled. Princely fortunes were made by the capitalists engaged in the fisheries, many of them securing from $60,000 to $100,000 of profits in a single season. Persons who commenced the business entirely destitute of capital shared in these enormous gains, and accumulated large fortunes in a short period. In 1814 the quantity of fish exported was over 1,200,000 quintals, of the value of more than $12,000,000. In 1815 the export was almost as large. But, if the war raised wages, it also immensely increased the price of all the necessaries and luxuries of life. Flour was £8 per barrel; pork £12 per barrel. The fishermen spent their wages lavishly at the stores of the merchants, never dreaming that the good times were not to last forever, or that a fearful commercial crash, destined to cause much suffering, was at hand.

10. During those years of prosperous fisheries and increasing population, from 1796 to 1814, improvements of various kinds were slowly working their way. But the old restrictive system was still maintained in full force, and prevented the people from cultivating the soil, making comfortable homes for themselves, and securing their independence. The vast wealth realized by the fisheries went to enrich other lands. None of it was spent in the improvement of the island, or for the promotion of civilization among its resident population. No other British colony was ever dealt with so harshly. Millions of money were lavished in promoting the settlement of Nova Scotia, New Brunswick, and Canada; but not only was encouragement denied to settlers in Newfoundland, but all grants of land were sternly refused.

11. Many of the governors who were appointed, and who held office for three or four years each, were enlightened and humane men, and quite alive to the evils of the system and the miseries which it caused. But they were naval officers, who resided only a few months each year in the island. Naturally they were inclined to sustain the old order of things which regarded the country as a fishing-station, and a training port for seamen, not as a home for a civilized community. They, therefore, strictly enforced the policy which reserved the shores of the island for the use of the migratory fishermen from England, and denied all applications for land grants.

12. As an illustration of the working of the system, two instances may be mentioned. In 1790 Governor Milbanke discovered that a house had been erected in St. John's without permission. He immediately issued orders to the sheriff to pull it down, declaring that no property in land would be allowed except it were actually employed in connection with the fishery. In 1799 Governor Waldegrave found, on his return from his winter sojourn in England, that a fence and two sheds had been put up during his absence. He sharply rebuked the sheriff for his laxity, and ordered both erections to be removed. Yet he was an intelligent, humane man, and was the first to institute charitable societies for the relief of the poor, with whose deplorable condition he showed much sympathy. He also did what he could to promote education, and he secured the erection of a new church in St. John's. But the governors of those days considered that loyalty to England obliged them to enforce the harsh system, however hardly it pressed on the people.

13. Good influences, however, were at work among the people, who had long been suffering from social disadvantages. In many of the smaller settlements successive generations had hitherto lived and died without education, or almost any religious instruction. It is not wonderful that, among a people so circumstanced, irreligion, immorality, and disorder should have prevailed, more or less. But now a change for the better commenced. Churches had been springing up in various localities; and, in connection with these, secular and Sunday schools were opened for the education of the young. Clergymen, both Protestant and Catholic, left the old country to minister to the spiritual wants of the long-neglected people. Amid hardships and privations of the severest kind these good men toiled with commendable devotion among their flocks. Under all these beneficial influences a striking change for the better was gradually effected.

14. A serious alarm was created, in the year 1800,

by the discovery of a mutinous plot among the soldiers stationed at St. John's, composing the Royal Newfoundland Regiment, which had been enlisted chiefly from among the populace. The conspirators appear to have had sympathizers and adherents among the more turbulent and ignorant of the lower classes, who were prepared to act in concert with the mutineers. Their plan was to desert with their arms, and, being joined with their friends outside, to plunder St. John's, and afterwards escape to the United States. Had the conspiracy not been detected in time, terrible results would have followed, involving robbery and assassination. The discovery of the plot was made by the Roman Catholic Bishop, Dr. O'Donnell, who promptly informed the commanding officer of the impending peril. Prompt measures were taken. The ringleaders among the soldiers were tried by court-martial and executed. The regiment was relieved by another from Halifax, and the alarm speedily subsided. All classes felt and acknowledged the debt of gratitude due to Bishop O'Donnell for his conduct on this occasion. To mark their sense of his patriotic conduct the British Government bestowed on him a pension of £50 per annum, an inadequate reward for such an important service.

15. During the administration of Governor Sir Erasmus Gower, which commenced in 1804, a very important improvement was effected in St. John's. Previous to this time the principal buildings of the town were huddled into a small space, extending around the margin of the harbour, and at no great distance from high-water mark, there being no permission to erect permanent dwellings elsewhere. Governor Gower succeeded in obtaining the consent of the British ministry to a new arrangement, by which the grounds near the

water were reserved for the purposes of a mercantile port; and the land higher up was sold, in small lots, for the erection of houses. The improvement of the town dates from this more liberal arrangement. The prohibition against building had led to the erection of wooden huts in a narrow space, and in such a way as to present a continual danger from fire. In one place, the thoroughfare was not more than six feet wide. All the streets were narrow, unpaved, and unlighted.

16. Thus the old system of prohibiting the erection of houses, without a written permission from the Governor, at last received its death-blow. Governor Sir John Thomas Duckworth, who arrived in 1810, carried out this great improvement, by leasing the ground around the harbour for wharves and sites for mercantile premises. At the close of his term of office he reported to the British government that the resident population had now so largely increased that the fisheries were mainly carried on by them, and that it was vain to attempt lessening their numbers or checking their increase. He recommended that all impediments to the cultivation of the soil should be removed, so that the population might provide for their wants by agriculture as well as fishing. His successor was authorized to carry out these suggestions; but he did so with a very niggardly hand. Small plots of ground, four acres in extent, were granted on short leases, and with a rent attached. There were no roads, and yet, under these unfavourable conditions, the applications for land were more numerous than could be met. It is evident that, with such restricted land-grants agriculture could make little progress. The illiberal policy continued still for more than twenty years; and was only effectually ended when the colony obtained a legislature and the power of self-government.

17. Governor Duckworth proved to be a ruler possessed of activity and intelligence. He made a voyage to the northern settlements and Labrador, in order to acquaint himself with the condition and wants of the people. He endeavoured to establish friendly relations with the Red Indians of the country ; but his efforts unfortunately failed. He established a hospital in St. John's, which proved to be a great boon to the poorer classes of the city and its suburbs. His memory is still deservedly held in respect.

18. The years 1805 and 1806 witnessed the introduction of two of the great resources of civilization, — a post-office and a newspaper. Previously, letters were sent by any casual conveyance ; now a postmaster was appointed, and merchant-vessels carried the mail-bags. The first newspaper was the " Royal Gazette." It was published by John Ryan, and is still in existence.

QUESTIONS FOR EXAMINATION ON CHAPTER XII.

1. What was the effect of Palliser's Act?

2. When did the American Revolution begin? How did it affect Newfoundland? How was the island defended?

3. When was the independence of the United States acknowledged? What good effects followed to Newfoundland?

4. What important proclamation did Governor Campbell issue in 1784? What was the result to Roman Catholics? What Catholic clergyman arrived?

5. When was the first Bishop of the Church of England appointed? Who planted Wesleyan Methodism? Give the date of Congregationalism?

6. What change did the Treaty of Versailles make?

7. What great improvement came in 1793? Who was the first Chief Justice? Mention what he did for the good of the people.

8. What great war began in 1793? Who invaded the island? What happened?

9. What effect had this war on the condition of the colony? Describe its prosperity. What emigrants arrived in 1814? What were the exports in 1814 and 1815?

10. What were the grievances of the people during this period?
11. Why did the Governors sustain the old order of things?
12. Mention some instances of restrictions in land grants.
13. What good influences were at work?
14. Give the particulars of the mutiny in 1800. Who discovered it? How was he rewarded?
15. What improvement came in 1804?
16. What report did Governor Duckworth make of the colony?
17. What did he do for the good of the country?
18. What improvements came in 1805 and 1806?

NOTES AND EXPLANATIONS. — CHAPTER XII.

French Fisheries in Newfoundland Waters. — The importance attached by France to these fisheries may be judged from the fact that, in fortifying Louisburg, in Cape Breton, she spent over a million sterling. "This," said Abbé Raynal, "was not thought too great a sum for the support of the fisheries, for securing the communication between France and Canada, for obtaining a security or retreat to ships in time of war, coming from the Southern islands." In the confusion which followed the French Revolution, bounties were discontinued, and in consequence, the number of French fishermen engaged in these fisheries fell from 15,000 in 1777, to 3,400 in 1793. Subsequently, they were abandoned almost entirely till the return of peace in 1814.

At the present time the number of French fishermen engaged in the Newfoundland Bank and Shore fisheries is over 7,000, and the average value of their catch is £280,000 sterling.

Chief-Justice Reeves. — He deservedly holds a first place among the benefactors of Newfoundland. His able "History" effectually opened the eyes of British statesmen to the evils of the existing system in the island; and by his personal, judicious efforts, he accomplished much good. Of the Fishing Admirals he said, "They are ever the servants of the merchants. Justice was not to be expected from them; and a poor planter or inhabitant, who was considered little better than a law-breaker in being such, had but a small chance of justice, in opposition to any great west-country merchant. They considered that Newfoundland was theirs, and that all the planters were to be spoiled, and devoured at their pleasure."

The term "planter" in Newfoundland means a sort of middle-man, who obtains supplies for the fisheries from the merchant, and employs fishermen to whom he distributes these supplies, in the locality where he resides. At the end of the season he sells the fish he has collected to the merchant, and pays the fishermen their wages. At first the merchants and their immediate servants were the only classes of persons engaged in the fisheries. Then a third class was added, called "Bye-boat keepers," who also kept a certain number of servants and were supplied by the merchants, to whom they sold the produce of their voyage. In course of time these became resident "planters."

Fires in the woods are very common in Newfoundland, and destroy an immense amount of timber. In the summer of 1812, which was unusually hot, Harbour Grace had a narrow escape from destruction by one of these fires which approached close to the town. The scene is said to have been one of terrific grandeur, as the flames leaped from thicket to thicket with a roaring noise and huge volumes of smoke. The inhabitants rushed out, and, by cutting semicircular spaces between the town and the blazing woods, with great difficulty, arrested the progress of the fire.

Colonization in Newfoundland.—The contrast between the treatment of Newfoundland and that of the neighbouring colonies is very striking. While capital, skill, and labour were directed to the improvement of the other colonies, the adventurers to Newfoundland extracted millions from its resources, without expending anything on its internal improvement. If only a portion of the wealth drawn from its fisheries had, at an early period, been spent in promoting the cultivation of the soil and opening up the interior, its now unoccupied wastes would long since have been covered with a prosperous population. But, while in Newfoundland the most strenuous efforts were made to prevent settlement and cultivation, in Nova Scotia money was lavished by the British Government in promoting colonization. Burke stated, in the House of Commons, that Nova Scotia had cost England £700,000. In 1749 the first settlers landed at Chebucto Harbour (now Halifax), and for their assistance Parliament voted £40,000 sterling. The settlement of Lunenburgh, Nova Scotia, in seven years, cost England £445,584. On roads, canals, mines, and other public works in Canada, millions were expended, while protective duties secured a monopoly for its products in English markets. Contrast with this the harsh treatment of the Newfoundland colonists, and the injury done to the fisheries by unwise concessions to the French. New Zealand and New South Wales present a similar contrast in the bountiful encouragement they received in their infancy.

The West Country Trade with Newfoundland.—The following extracts from an article which appeared in "The Western Times," an Exeter newspaper, in 1872, refer to the time when the fisheries were carried on from England: "The places nearest to us most engaged in the trade of Newfoundland, towards the end of the last century and the beginning of the present, were Teignmouth, Shaldon, Torquay, Dartmouth. Many old hands will remember the large concern carried on by the house of Newman, at Dartmouth, from which has sprung the Baronet of Mamhead House; and also the names of Job,

Codner, and Hunt. At Torquay there were the Stabbs, Prowses, and others; at Teignmouth, Warren; at Shaldon there were the Rowes, Wilkings, Harveys, and divers others, who owned a considerable fleet of craft employed in fishing on the Banks, and in carrying the cured fish to the ports of Spain, Portugal, and the Mediterranean, and Great Britain. It was one of the ways by which the country side was relieved of its redundant rustic population. The young fellows who had a little pluck in them left the mattock and shovel, and betook them to the hook and line. Many Devonshire men spent their lives in going annually to the Newfoundland fishing work, either on the Banks or in large boats along the shore, from March till November. The return of the vessels in November was a time of great anxiety to hundreds of wives and families in South Devon, as well as to the merchant-adventurers concerned therein. To them the year's luck in cod-fishing was everything, and the arrivals of the returning vessels, in this dreary month, an exciting time.

"Employment was given by the Newfoundland trade, in the ship-building yards, to rope, sail, and net makers, and to the manufacturers of all kinds of clothing. The cordage, sail, and net making was, for the most part, carried off by Bridport. Nor has Exeter been without its interest in Newfoundland matters. The manufacture of the hooks used in the cod-fishing was carried on here,—among the last, by a family in Fore street, among whom it appears to have been hereditary. Serges, woven in Exeter, were largely exported to the Peninsula by the vessels which carried the cured cod, and other fish to the Catholic countries of Spain and Portugal,—the fish for food on fast days, the serges to clothe the monks.

"The change that has since come may beget a feeling something stronger than surprise; for not only is the trade, the shipping, and all the local interest vanished, but a generation has arisen that seems to have forgotten how much codfish and seal-skins contributed to raise the condition of several very pretty and flourishing towns, not to mention the fortunes of private men."

CHRONOLOGICAL SUMMARY.—CHAPTERS XI. AND XII.

A.D.
1756. Seven Years' War commenced.
1758. Second capture of Louisburg.
1759. Quebec taken by Wolfe.
1760. George III. commenced to reign.
1762. St. John's, Newfoundland, taken by the French.
1763. Treaty of Paris.
   Labrador attached to Newfoundland.

1764.	Customs and Navigation Laws introduced, Newfoundland.
1774.	First American Congress.
	Battle of Lexington.
1775.	Battle of Bunker Hill.
1776.	Declaration of American Independence.
1777.	Battle of Brandywine.
1778.	France acknowledged independence of United States.
1780.	Gordon Riots in London.
1782.	England acknowledged Independence of United States.
1783.	Treaty of Versailles.
	William Pitt the younger, Prime Minister of England.
1784.	Religious freedom established in Newfoundland.
1788.	Impeachment of Warren Hastings.
1789.	French Revolution.
1793.	Supreme Court established in Newfoundland.
1797.	Spain and England at war.
1798.	Rebellion in Ireland.
	Battle of the Nile.
1800.	Mutiny in the garrison detected at St. John's.
1801.	Union of Great Britain and Ireland.
	Battle of the Baltic.
1804.	Napoleon Bonaparte Emperor.
1805.	Post-office introduced, Newfoundland.
	Battles of Trafalgar and Austerlitz.
1806.	First newspaper published in Newfoundland.
1809.	Battles of Corunna and Talavera.
1812.	United States declared war against England.
	Retreat of Napoleon from Moscow.
	Americans invaded Canada.
1813.	Battle of Leipsic.
1814.	Battle of Lundy's Lane, Canada.
	Abdication of Napoleon.
	First Treaty of Paris.
	Treaty of Ghent.
1815.	Battle of Waterloo.
1815.	Second Treaty of Paris.

EMINENT AUTHORS.

Gibbon; Hume; Burns; Edmund Burke; Cowper; Junius; Adam Smith Keats; Shelley; Byron; Scott.

CHAPTER XIII.

FROM 1814 TO 1861.

COMMERCIAL DISASTERS.

FIRST OF 1816–17. — PAUPERISM. — FIRST ROADS IN 1825. — REPRESENTATIVE GOVERNMENT GRANTED. — CONDITION OF THE FISHERIES IN 1832. — POLITICAL DISTURBANCES. — CAUSES OF THESE CONFLICTS. — PUBLIC IMPROVEMENTS. — GREAT FIRE OF 1846. — " RESPONSIBLE GOVERNMENT" GRANTED IN 1854. — FIRST ATLANTIC CABLE IN 1858. — VISIT OF THE PRINCE OF WALES IN 1860. — POLITICAL TROUBLES.

1. We have seen how prosperous were the fisheries during the long European wars which followed the French Revolution. The price of fish trebled; and all the fish-markets of Europe were supplied from Newfoundland. Neither French nor American fishermen were to be found on the Banks. Great numbers of emigrants were attracted to the island by the high rate of wages, and the population rapidly increased. Immense fortunes were quickly made by the capitalists. The middle classes, too, increased in wealth and numbers. No one dreamed that this artificial and exceptional prosperity could not last, or imagined that the sunshine was soon to be overclouded and disaster and ruin to descend on the community. In prosperity no provision was made for the dark days of adversity.

2. The battle of Waterloo, in 1815, brought the great European conflict to a close, and peace was reëstablished by the Treaty of Paris. By this treaty the French right of fishing on the Banks and shores of the island was restored to its former footing. Americans were also allowed extended privileges of fishing in British waters. Both French and Americans at once established a system of bounties to encourage their own fishermen; and, at the same time, by high duties, prevented the admission of Newfoundland fish into their own markets. The result was a rapid extension of the French and American fisheries. Newfoundland had now to compete, in the fish-consuming countries, with Frenchmen and Americans, whose governments paid them a liberal sum for every quintal of fish caught, over and above the price for which it sold. The British government granted no bounties; and thus the Newfoundland fishermen had to compete with the others on very unequal terms.

3. The consequence of the new condition of things was that the price of fish fell speedily from forty-five to twelve shillings per quintal. This brought on a commercial crash, at the close of 1815, involving a large proportion of the merchants and planters in bankruptcy and ruin. Numbers of the large mercantile firms became hopelessly involved, and were unable to pay their creditors. Others, who were not insolvent, became so disheartened that they realized whatever property remained, and left the country. Only a few managed to weather the storm, and these were greatly reduced in their means of carrying on business. No less than nine hundred cases, arising out of extensive failures, came before the civil courts. Losses by bankruptcies amounted to a million pounds sterling. The middle and working classes suffered with the rest. There was little use made of banks in those days, and planters and fishermen were in the habit of leaving their savings, during prosperous years, in the hands of the merchants, for safekeeping. The bankruptcy of the merchants swept away

all their hardly earned savings. It is calculated that the working-classes lost, in this way, the large sum of £400,000, a great part of what they had accumulated in the late prosperous period.

4. These were dark and trying days. Supplies for the fisheries were suddenly cut off or greatly lessened. Multitudes were thus deprived of the means of earning their bread. In many instances the wages earned during the summer of 1815 were not paid to the fishermen, owing to the insolvency of their employers. A large population had been attracted by the prosperity of previous years, and these could not now be sustained in the depressed condition of the fisheries. Large numbers were left unemployed, and became dependent on public charity. It was absolutely necessary to remove some of them. At the public expense many of the most destitute were shipped to Ireland. Over a thousand were sent to Halifax.

5. Such was the state of affairs at the close of 1815, and this was but the beginning of disasters. On the 12th of February of the following year, 1816, a terrible fire broke out in St. John's, during the night, when a heavy gale was blowing. It was a night of terrors. The flames, fanned by a furious wind, spread with inconceivable rapidity among wooden houses, huddled together without any stone or brick partitions, or any provision for safety. Hundreds had barely time to escape from their dwellings with scarcely any covering, and stood shivering in the piercing blasts; while all they possessed was perishing before their eyes, and they were left without a shelter. No less than 120 houses were destroyed, and 1,500 persons left without a home. The loss of property was estimated at £100,000.

6. The fisheries of 1817 were disastrous failures, and

the price of fish was very low. The sufferings of the poor fishermen were terrible, although every effort was made to alleviate their distress. Food-riots broke out, and men with arms in their hands, rendered desperate by starvation, demanded relief from the magistrates, and broke into the merchants' stores and carried off provisions. Order, however, was soon reëstablished. The British Parliament sent relief to the distressed colony, and private charity was active.

7. But now arrived what seemed to be the crowning calamity, to complete the wretchedness of the people. On the 7th of November, 1817, another destructive fire broke out in St. John's, and in a few hours 13 mercantile establishments, 140 dwelling-houses, besides stores and wharves, were destroyed, and 1,100 persons were left without homes. The loss of property was nearly £500,000 sterling. Many of those involved in the former fire were severe sufferers now; and numbers of the most respectable inhabitants lost all their property. The long and dreary winter was before them. They were congratulating themselves on the fact that one-half of the town was still left to shelter them, when only a fortnight after, on the 21st of November, the terrible cry of "Fire!" again startled them from their slumbers. Before the flames could be arrested, 56 houses, with several stores and wharves, were burned. These fires left 2,000 persons houseless, many of whom had lost all they possessed.

8. Scenes of heart-rending distress followed. When news of these calamitous events spread, sympathy was at once awakened, and help speedily arrived. Provisions were despatched from Halifax to save the inhabitants from starvation. The generous people of Boston loaded a vessel with provisions of various kinds, which proved a

most welcome gift. The British government sent prompt and liberal aid. The Governor, the merchants, and the wealthier classes exerted themselves to relieve the wants of the more destitute portion of the people. A number of those had been left without homes removed to the out-harbours, and some went to other countries.

9. Though there were a few instances of disorder arising from the pressure of want and misery, the people, on the whole, met their calamities with fortitude and patience. It was not long till the dark hour became brighter, and began to pass away. The seal and cod fisheries of 1818 were unusually successful. All over the commercial world prosperity began to revive. The price of fish in the home and foreign markets rose considerably. The people who had suffered so sorely took fresh courage, and soon industrial activity was everywhere visible. The inhabitants of St. John's set to work to clear away the blackened ruins; and, phœnix-like, the town soon rose from its ashes. The streets were widened, precautions against fire were taken, and more substantial dwellings replaced the old wooden structures which had furnished fuel to former conflagrations.

10. Admiral Pickmore had been Governor during those calamitous years. He was the first resident Governor, — the practice formerly being that the governors arrived in July or August, and left for England in October or November. Henceforward they were required to reside in the island. Governor Pickmore died in St. John's in February, 1818, and his remains were sent to England for interment. He was succeeded in July of the same year by Sir Charles Hamilton.

11. St. John's was not the only place which suffered by fire. In 1816 a fire broke out in Carbonear which destroyed sixteen houses and much property. The Metho-

dist church was one of the buildings consumed in this fire. The parish church of Harbour Grace, which had recently been enlarged, was burned towards the close of the same year.

12. Though the country had begun to recover from these severe blows yet the effects of those three years of adversity were felt long afterwards, and greatly retarded the progress of the colony. The losses sustained by the working-classes reduced many of them to a state of poverty; and each winter season, owing to partial failures of the fisheries, numbers became dependent on public charity. Relief of this kind, extended to able-bodied men, had a demoralizing effect, destroying their self-respect and self-reliance, and rendering them reckless and improvident. The governing powers, in after years, found great difficulty in dealing with this constantly recurring pauperism, which became a heavy burden on the revenue of the country. Still, it is not to be wondered at that these public calamities should have created a serious amount of poverty. Almost universal bankruptcy had deranged business from one end of the island to the other, and an enormous amount of capital had been swept away by fires. But all difficulties were met with spirit and energy, and were eventually overcome.

13. Up to this time the people had no voice in the management of their own affairs. The power of the governors was absolute, and their rule a despotism. They were generally inclined to sustain the old order of things, and, as a rule, were opposed to changes and improvements which the altered circumstances of the colony demanded. A desire for self-government now took possession of many minds. In 1821 an agitation was begun for the introduction of such institutions as would confer on the people the power of making their own laws,

and, through their chosen representatives, regulating all matters affecting their well-being. Such a desire was a proof of advancing intelligence and self-reliance among the people. At first the British government would not listen to the petitions for local self-government. The supporters of the old despotic system in the colony were opposed to it; and it required an agitation of ten years to secure this right.

14. The administration of justice was greatly improved, in 1824, by an act of the British Parliament which provided that the Supreme Court should be held by the Chief-Justice and two assistant judges. The island was divided into three districts, in each of which a Circuit Court was appointed to be held annually, by one of the judges, from the decisions of which an appeal to the Supreme Court was permitted. A Court of Civil Jurisdiction was also instituted for Labrador. This arrangement secured for the people the pure administration of justice, on the principles of English law, — one of the greatest blessings.

15. In 1825 Sir Thomas Cochrane was appointed Governor. By his commission it was ordered that a Council should divide with him the responsibility of his government. Before this time governors had been sole rulers, acting on their own discretion. This Council, nominated by the crown, consisted of the three judges and the commander of the garrison stationed at St. John's. It constituted a decided improvement on the old despotic system, and proved to be the first step towards government by representatives chosen by the people.

16. Sir Thomas Cochrane proved to be an excellent Governor. He made liberal grants of land, though his leases contained unwise restrictions. He saw the necessity of roads, if agriculture was to make any progress. His government was rendered memorable by the construction of the first roads in the island. It speaks volumes for the injustice with which the colony had been treated, when, notwithstanding all the wealth drawn from its fisheries, two hundred and forty-two years elapsed from its annexation to the British Crown, by Sir Humphrey Gilbert, till the construction of the first road. One of Governor Cochrane's roads extended to Portugal Cove, nine miles distant from St. John's; another to Torbay, and another to Waterford Bridge. Along these roads farms were speedily laid off; neat cottages and farm-houses were erected, and cultivation advanced. A foundation was thus laid for future improvements; and people learned by experience the value of roads. Governor Cochrane also commenced and completed a handsome Government House in St. John's, at a cost of £30,000, which amount was furnished by the British Government.

17. Meantime, as the ideas of the people continued to advance, and the prospects of the country brightened, the desire for local self-government began to pervade the minds of all classes. Public meetings on the subject were held; petitions to the British Parliament poured in; and the force of public opinion at last became irresistible. In 1832, the great boon of Representative Government was bestowed on Newfoundland. The island was divided into nine electoral districts, each of which was to have one or more representatives, according to population. Every man who had occupied a house for a year preceding the day of election, and who was twenty-one years of age, was entitled to a vote. The year 1833 marked a new era in the history of the colony. On the first day of that year, the Governor, with all due pomp

and ceremony, opened the first Local Legislature. The people had now obtained the power of making their own laws, expending their revenue, and guiding their own affairs. Such a power, once granted, could never be permanently withdrawn. It might be abused, and be attended by heavy drawbacks, but the advantages were altogether in favor of self-government. It has been found to be the great school for developing the energies of a free people, and promoting national progress.

18. The long-drawn battle between the merchant-adventurers, who carried on the fishery from England, and the resident population was over long since. The hardy settlers were conquerors, and now held the fishery entirely in their own hands. The English Bank fishery declined rapidly after the close of the last war with France. Before that date nearly four hundred vessels fitted out in England were employed in the Bank fishery, and two-thirds of the fish exported were taken on the Banks. Then came a sudden change and a fall in the price of fish. The English could not compete with the French and American Bank fishermen, who were sustained by large national bounties which gave them a premium on the fish caught. In the resident fishermen of the island, who carried on the fisheries in boats around the shore, the English Bankers had also formidable rivals, who gradually gained the superiority. The English Bank fishery dwindled away, from these two causes. In 1832 only a dozen small schooners prosecuted the Bank fishery; and in a few years more it became totally extinct. The Newfoundland fishermen, living near the fishing-grounds, were able to compete successfully with the French and Americans, who had to make long and expensive voyages to the Banks. As their numbers increased their annual catch of fish improved, till they exported yearly over a

million quintals of fish, taken around the shores of the island and on the coast of Labrador. The average catch was thus equal to that of the palmy days of the English Bank fishery. There was this further advantage, that the wealth now amassed in the fisheries was less likely to be carried away to other lands, and that more of it would remain among those whose labours had won it, and who would employ it in the improvement of the country.

19. Newfoundland, having passed through periods of oppression and trial, had now attained to a position of freedom; and its Legislature, composed of representatives chosen by the people, was the safeguard of its liberties. The people were no longer subject to the knavish and despotic "fishing-admirals," or to the quarter-deck mandates of their successors, the captains and commodores of the royal navy, who regarded the inhabitants as "subject to naval discipline." The rule of a few merchants, armed with the ordinances of "the Lords of Trade and Plantations," who once controlled the whole business of the island, and even the domestic life of the residents, had closed long since. The boon of self-government placed the destinies of the people in their own hands, and awakened new life and self-reliance among them. They now began to feel that for themselves, their children, and their country a brighter and better future was opening up.

20. They had yet to learn, however, through bitter experience, that freedom is a gift which may be readily abused, and that its benefits can only be enjoyed when moderation, intelligence, and morality guide the conduct of its possessors. The years which followed the introduction of representative government in Newfoundland were, unhappily, marked by strife and bitter contentions, leading to social discords, and, at times, to scenes of turbulence and disorder, in connection with the elections of representatives. This was the price which had to be paid for liberty, and it proved to be heavy. To understand the causes of these troubles it must be remembered that the population of the colony was composed of two great bodies, differing in race and religion, whose numbers at this time were nearly equal. Half of the inhabitants were Roman Catholics of Irish descent, among whom it might naturally be expected memories of Old-World strifes, wrongs, and oppressions would be rife. The other half were Protestants, of English descent, who were, for a long time, accustomed to hold the ascendency. These were headed by a wealthy mercantile class, who were not disposed to give up their time-honoured claim to rule. Further, as we have seen, Catholics had been, at one time, harshly persecuted; and, though this had ceased long since, the memories of old wrongs and grievances were not yet effaced.

21. When, then, representative government was introduced old jealousies and distrusts were revived. Each party dreaded the political superiority of the other, and each sought to gain the controlling power. Religion was unhappily dragged into the political arena. A licentious press stimulated the strife, and the worst passions were evoked. The peace of social and commercial life was disturbed by the political excitement of the hour. Some outrages, which were perpetrated by the more ignorant and turbulent, added fuel to the flame. Over this period of political and religious contention it is better to draw a veil, and consign the memory of it to oblivion. It produced only evil results, rancour, hatred, and evil passions and seriously retarded the progress of the country.

22. It should be understood that these contentions were only seriously felt at election seasons, which re-

curred at intervals of four years; and that the stormy passions thus evoked quickly subsided, and that the people forgot their differences, and lived in harmony. Apart from these political turmoils the population was orderly, and serious crime was almost unknown. Gradually both parties learned the folly of such proceedings and the injury they entailed. Each learned to respect better the rights of the others, and to recognize the equality which the constitution established. As kindly feelings prevailed a good understanding was restored, and old strifes were forgotten. In the present day the love of country is gradually rising above these strifes and contentions, and the people are learning that their true happiness is to be attained by living together peacefully, and labouring together to promote the interests of their common country, and to secure for it a high place among the rising communities of the New World. We can hardly expect that these political and sectarian strifes will disappear all at once. They have, unhappily, reappeared at intervals since the times we are describing, and always with injurious results. But, as intelligence spreads, and higher feelings are called into play, they will disappear forever.

23. Notwithstanding these political disturbances the benefits of self-government were soon felt by the passing of many useful measures in the Legislature. An act was passed for the erection of light-houses at various points along the coast. An annual vote of money for the promotion of education was adopted. An academy for the promotion of a higher education, was established in St. John's. In 1834 Sir Thomas Cochrane was succeeded by Captain Prescott, as Governor. Liberal grants of land were made to hundreds of poor families. The House of Assembly voted £30,000 for roads and bridges.

24. In 1841 Sir John Harvey was appointed governor. He used enlightened and energetic efforts to promote agriculture and the settlement of the country. He founded an agricultural society, which accomplished much good. The Legislature appropriated £40,000 for roads and bridges,— a proof of the wonderful revolution people's ideas had undergone since the days when the country was pronounced unfit for settlement, and only valuable as a rock on which fish might be dried. To remove all impediments to agriculture an act was passed which secured the sale of all crown lands, at a moderate price, to settlers. This proved to be an invaluable boon to the country. Other improvements followed. In 1840 a mail sailing-packet was appointed to ply fortnightly between St. John's and Halifax; and, in 1844, this was followed by the first steam-packet bearing a mail for Newfoundland.

25. While the country was thus prospering and improving, another terrible calamity from fire, greater by far than any of the preceding visitations, fell upon the capital, inflicting terrible losses, and for a time checked all progress. On the 9th of June, 1846, a fire broke out in the western end of St. John's which swept everything before it, and, before night closed in, three-fourths of a wealthy and populous city were a smoking mass of ruins. The rapidity of the terrible conflagration was owing in part to a high wind which prevailed at the time, and which hurled the blazing brands far and wide, and also to the fact that the greater part of the houses were wooden. Even the mercantile establishments, built substantially of stone and brick, presented no barrier to the progress of the fierce conflagration, and, with a single exception, they were totally destroyed. Nearly all the public buildings except Government House perished.

The Post-office, Savings-bank, Bank of British North America, Custom-house, Police-office, Exchange Buildings, Ordnance Store, and many others were burned to the ground. To add to the terrors of the scene, while the red tongues of flame were leaping from street to street, the huge oil-vats on the side of the harbour took fire. Liquid flames spread over the whole surface of the water, and set fire to a number of vessels. Before the day closed twelve thousand people were homeless, and property valued at a million pounds sterling was destroyed.

26. Still there was no abject despair among the people, though their condition was sufficiently disheartening. Vessels were at once despatched for provisions. When news of the terrible calamity reached England a sum of £5,000 was sent for immediate relief, and Parliament voted £25,000 more. To this was added a very large sum collected in the churches, under the sanction of a letter from the Queen to the Archbishops of Canterbury and York. The neighbouring colonies sent liberal contributions. Cheered by this generous sympathy, the inhabitants at once set to work to rebuild their city. A law was enacted prohibiting wooden houses in the business part of the town, and enforcing increased width of the streets. Some years afterwards an abundant supply of water was introduced; so that St. John's is now as secure against fire as any other city of the New World. A recurrence of such a terrible conflagration as that of June 9, 1846, may be regarded as impossible. A much handsomer city has arisen on the ruins of the old, having improved sanitary arrangements, and abundant supply of excellent water and safeguards against fire.

27. Another public calamity was destined to mark the memorable year 1846. On the 19th of September a storm of unexampled severity swept over the island, causing

an immense destruction of shipping-houses, fishing-stages and flakes, boats, and bridges, and in many instances engulfing the fruits of the fishermen's toils during the previous summer. These two calamities, in a single year, were a serious drawback to the prosperity of the colony for a long time.

28. Sir Gaspard Le Marchant was appointed Governor in 1847. Previous to his arrival, a strong agitation had sprung up in favour of what is known as "Responsible Government," a form of which had been already conceded to all the other North American colonies. The object was to attain a more complete power of self-government than the Constitution of 1832 had secured. The appointments to the principal offices in the colony were still held by the Crown, and were disposed of by the Governor and his Council. Under "Responsible Government," all such appointments were to be at the disposal of the party which commanded a majority in the Legislature. It was thus simply government according to the wishes of the people, as expressed in the choice of their representatives, and the executive were made responsible to the House of Assembly. This very reasonble demand was resisted for a time; but at length conceded in 1854. Charles Darling, Esq., was sent out as the successor of Ker B. Hamilton, Esq., to introduce "Responsible Government."

29. The British Government entered into an agreement with the French, in 1857, for the purpose of settling disputed points in connection with the Newfoundland fisheries. The terms of this agreement, when made known, were regarded as very unfavourable to the interests of Newfoundland. A storm of opposition arose, and delegates were sent to remonstrate with the British Government. The clauses in the agreement which gave offence

were at once withdrawn, and the Secretary of State for the colonies, in a despatch to the Governor, gave the assurance that "the consent of the community of Newfoundland is regarded by Her Majesty's Government as an essential preliminary to any modification of their territorial or maritime rights." This, of course, was a complete guarantee of the power of the colony to regulate its own affairs, existing treaties being duly respected.

30. "Responsible government" worked well. Education was fostered and extended; more light-houses were erected to protect the mariners around a dangerous coast; steam communication, both internal and foreign, was improved; a telegraph line was built across the island. An increasing revenue enabled the Legislature to undertake these works of public utility.

31. The year 1858 was marked by a great and important historic event. A sub-marine cable was successfully laid from the Irish coast to the eastern shores of Newfoundland, a distance of 1,640 miles. On the 5th of August, 1858, the great enterprise was accomplished; and the first telegraphic message between the Old World and the New was flashed across the island which Cabot had discovered three hundred and sixty-one years before. The fine geographical situation of Newfoundland, reaching out so far towards Europe, presented facilities for establishing communication by telegraph between the two hemispheres. Soundings previously taken in the Atlantic had proved that between Newfoundland and Ireland there is a great level submarine plain, a thousand miles wide, admirably adapted by the hand of Nature for the reception of the cable which constituted a nerve of communication between the two worlds. But for these facilities such communication might have been delayed for many years.

32. In 1860 His Royal Highness the Prince of Wales visited St. John's on his way to Canada. He met with a most loyal and enthusiastic welcome from all classes of the people.

33. The year 1861 was darkened by political commotions, in which the old animosities, which had been long dormant, were once more revived. A change of government had taken place, and general elections were held in April, 1861. In a work like the present, designed mainly for the use of the young, it would not be profitable or desirable to dwell upon the scenes of tumult and violence which unhappily took place. It is enough to mention that in Harbour Main one life was lost, and that in St. John's, during the suppression of a riot by the military, who were called out, three persons were killed and several wounded. Harbour Grace also was the scene of serious disturbances. The fact that for more than twenty years afterwards no similar scenes occurred at elections, may be hopefully regarded as a proof that a better spirit is prevailing, and that old animosities will gradually be forgotten.

QUESTIONS FOR EXAMINATION ON CHAPTER XIII.

1. In what condition was the country in 1814?
2. What effect had the Treaty of Paris on the fisheries? What advantage had French and Americans in the fishery?
3. When did the commercial crisis arrive? What caused it? Describe its effects on Newfoundland. What was the loss of the middle and working classes?
4. How did the fishermen suffer? What was done to remove some of them?
5. Describe the fire of 1816.
6. What disturbances followed?
7. Describe the losses by the fires of 1817. How many persons were houseless?
8. Who sent relief to the people?

9. How did the people bear their troubles? What improvements in the town were made on rebuilding?
10. Who was the first resident Governor?
11. What other towns suffered by fire?
12. What injurious effects followed the losses by fire?
13. What change in the form of government was now asked for?
14. What beneficial change in the Supreme Court came in 1824?
15. Who was Governor in 1825? What change was made in the form of government at that date?
16. When were roads first made? Where did the first roads reach to?
17. When was representative government granted? What was its effect? Who obtained votes?
18. What was the change made in the mode of conducting the fisheries? Was it beneficial? What destroyed the Bank Fishery?
19. How did disturbances arise from the introduction of representative government?
20. What divided the people and caused contentions? What evils were caused? What is the duty of people in order to preserve peace?
21. Mention improvements under representative government?
22. Under Sir John Harvey's government what improvements took place?
23. What calamity happened in St. John's in 1846? Describe the fire. What buildings were burned? What was the loss?
24. What relief was sent?
25. What injuries were done by the storm of 1846?
26. What is "Responsible Government," and when was it granted?
27. Give an account of the Convention about the fisheries in 1857.
28. What improvements followed Responsible Government?
29. What great event happened in 1858?
30. What marked 1861?
31. Describe the troubles in the elections of 1861.

NOTES AND EXPLANATIONS.—CHAPTER XIII.

Commercial Panic of 1815-17.—The sufferings of the people during the commercial disasters which followed the close of the French war, in 1815, aggravated as they were by three successive conflagrations in St. John's, were terrible. The high wages during the prosperous years had attracted large numbers of emigrants; and these continued to arrive during 1815, when the collapse in the fish-trade occurred. Famishing multitudes crowded St. John's in the following winter.

Captain Buchan, the officer in charge of the troops, put his men on short rations, and drew from the commissariat stores 500 tierces of flour to be baked into biscuit, which was doled out to the starving applicants. The merchants and wealthier inhabitants did all in their power to relieve the wants of the people. Their own stock of provisions was nearly exhausted, and their purses drained by such constant contributions as were called for. The spring of 1817 was dismal in the extreme. Enormous ice-fields around the coast stopped navigation for three months, and the sealing-vessels were so late in getting to sea that they returned with only 37,000 seals,—a poor return for their labours. The summer of that year was almost as dismal as the winter had been. The catch of codfish was small, and the price low. Multitudes were unemployed. Then came the terrible fires of November, 1817, and the direst sufferings among the people. From the outports came piteous appeals to the Governor for aid to save the lives of the starving inhabitants. The winter was one of the severest on record. The harbour of St. John's was frozen to the very entrance, the ice being several feet in thickness. It was at this critical time that the benevolent people of Boston, hearing of the dire distress in Newfoundland, raised a liberal subscription, and freighted a vessel with provisions for the relief of the sufferers. Fortunately, this vessel arrived in the middle of January, before the ice had closed navigation. She had on board 174 barrels of flour, 125 bags of meal, 11 tierces of rice, 27 barrels and 963 bags of bread. The whole was consigned to Governor Pickmore, to be distributed among the poor.

In acknowledging the timely offering the Governor said: "I confess myself unable to express in adequate terms, on behalf of those whose relief has been the object of the humane consideration of the inhabitants of Boston, the feelings which their generous act has excited. Individually I desire to offer my warmest acknowledgments to them, and shall not fail to communicate to His Majesty's government this spontaneous act of liberality, which, in its effects, I trust, will tend to increase and cement more firmly the relations of friendship which now so happily subsist between the two nations."

The foregoing words were written by Admiral Pickmore only a month before his death. He was the first governor who resided in the island during the winter. He was well advanced in years; and the troubles and anxieties of his position during those trying times wore out his strength. He died on the 24th of February, 1818. His remains, after lying for a time in the vault of the church, were placed on board His Majesty's sloop "Fly," with every mark of respect from the inhabitants, whose gratitude he had won by his untiring efforts to mitigate their sufferings.

This took place on the 10th of March. So intense was the frost, as has been already stated, that, though several hundred men were employed in cutting a passage through the ice in the harbour, for the "Fly" and other vessels which were ready for sea, three weeks were spent before the object was accomplished. The ice was from three to five feet thick, and the distance to cut the channel was about a mile. The "Fly" reached England in twenty-eight days.

The sealing-vessels made their way through these ice-channels, and soon returned well loaded with seals. An abundant cod-fishery followed, as generally happens after a severe winter, and the products brought much better prices. Hope revived in the breasts of the much-enduring people, and they went to work with renewed energies. The rich resources of the fisheries and their own native pluck and energy were such that calamities, however severe, could only prove temporary in their effects. Prosperity began to dawn, and their sufferings were forgotten.

It is curious to note the line of action taken by the merchant-adventurers who still carried on the fishery from England at this critical time. They still retained their old hostility to a population resident in the island, and were as jealous as ever of its interference with their monopoly. When the commercial crash took place they brought the distressed condition of the colony before the British House of Commons, and a select committee was appointed to investigate matters. Before this committee the merchants appeared, and asked that either a bounty should be given them to enable them to compete, on equal terms, with the French and Americans; or that the principal part of the inhabitants of Newfoundland, then numbering 70,000, should be transported to Canada and the Lower Provinces. This removal of the inhabitants had been their favourite remedy for the relief of the fisheries for ages before. In 1670 it is on record that "the merchants, owners, and masters of ships, and inhabitants of the western parts of the kingdom, adventurers to Newfoundland, petitioned Charles II., that the resident inhabitants and their families, then amounting to 3,171, should be removed to Jamaica, St. Christopher's, or some others of His Majesty's plantations." The "Merry Monarch" declined to carry out this humane suggestion; and now the descendants of the same "adventurers" actually repeated the proposal in 1817, when 70,000 people would have to be deported. Of course the House of Commons paid no attention to this outrageous demand, nor did they give a bounty to the merchants, which it was their real object to gain. They wisely left the colonists to grapple with their difficulties, and to conquer them by their own industry and perseverance. The consequence was that the fishery from England, by the merchant-adventurers, declined rapidly, and finally ceased, while that carried on from the shores of the island expanded and prospered, and, with the aid derived from agriculture, mining, and other resources, now sustains a population of 197,589.

Cultivation of the Soil.—The "merchant-adventurers" were never weary in repeating to the British Government that the soil of the island was utterly unfit for cultivation. Their object was to prevent settlement, and, for this purpose, to obtain from the government enactments prohibiting any enclosures of land. It was naturally said, if nature has already prohibited cultivation and doomed the island to barrenness, why need human laws raise further difficulties? As a specimen of the mercantile view of the matter we may quote the words of a Mr. George Kempt, a merchant, who was examined before the Parliamentary Committee of 1817. He said: "The island is composed of rock of granite and slate, with a very small surface of soil; in many places none at all, and *in very few above two or three inches.* The only places where there is any quantity of soil sufficient for cultivation *are the bogs;* but these cannot be drained. There is no limestone in the island, and no source of manure except a little sea-weed or the refuse of the fish. I beg, therefore, to suggest how much more eligible it would be for Government to carry the inhabitants" (at this time 70,000 in number) "to New Brunswick or Upper Canada." This veracious gentleman wanted to keep the island as a rock on which the servants of west-country merchants might dry fish, and to build up handsome fortunes for their employers.

Only twenty-five years afterwards, Sir John Harvey became governor. He had enjoyed a large experience in the neighbouring provinces, and, in addressing the Legislature in 1843, he said: "Here I will not deny myself the satisfaction of recording this public declaration of my conviction, derived from such observation and information as a residence in the island for upwards of a year has enabled me to acquire: that both as respects climate and agricultural capabilities Newfoundland, in many respects, need not shrink from a comparison with the most favoured provinces of British America. Its summers, though short, enjoy an extraordinary degree of vegetative power, which only requires to be duly taken advantage of; its winters are neither unusually long nor severe, and its autumnal seasons are as open and as fine as those of any of the surrounding colonies. In point of rich, natural grasses no part of British North America produces greater abundance. Newfoundland, in fact, appears to me to be calculated to become essentially a rich grazing country; and its varied agricultural resources appear only to require roads and settlements to force them into highly remunerative developments."

Later still came the geological survey under Mr. Murray, who declared that, in the principal valleys alone, there were three millions of acres of land well adapted for settlement, without taking into account areas fitted for grazing, which were of very large extent. And yet for a long period these mercantile monopolists were able to dupe the British government and people, until it became a settled belief that this large island, with a healthy climate and good soil, situated in a temperate latitude, presented insurmountable obstacles to agriculture.

It is but justice to state that the pioneer of agriculture in Newfoundland, in 1806, was Dr. William Carson, a native of Scotland, who for many years practised as a physician in St. John's, and was succeeded by his son, Dr. Samuel Carson. He courageously denounced the iniquitous laws which prohibited the cultivation of the soil, and by tongue and pen assailed the venerable system. He ran no small risk of being transported for his temerity, which, in those days, was regarded as treason against the government and mercantocracy. He persevered, however; declared that the soil was equal to that of his native Scotland, and would well repay cultivation. He was regarded as a visionary, and subjected to ridicule and the coarsest abuse. But he lived to see his views approved by a large majority. In 1819 he obtained from the governor a grant of a tract of waste land near St. John's, where he cleared and cultivated a valuable farm, and practically illustrated his doctrines. Two other agricultural pioneers may be mentioned: Mr. H. P. Thomas, a merchant, in 1827 cleared 250 acres, four miles from St. John's, and occupied it several years, until it repaid the whole of his outlay, when he leased it to a Scotch farmer, who is said to have cleared £4,000 during his occupancy. Mr. Robert Pack, merchant, of Carbonear, also obtained a grant of waste land, a mile from that town, which he brought to a state of excellent cultivation. These good examples stirred up the fishing population to enter on the cultivation of the soil, and the enclosure and reclamation of land rapidly advanced. It must be remembered, too, that these experiments were made near St. John's, where the soil is, perhaps, the poorest in the island. Now, by cultivation, the whole country round is transformed into smiling farms and covered with homesteads. When so much can be done with the poorest soil, what may be expected when the fertile valleys of the interior, where the harsh winds from the Atlantic are not felt, and where a higher temperature prevails, are occupied and cultivated? The climate of the interior and of the western coast is unaffected by the Arctic current, which chills the eastern shores, and is much more favourable for growing and ripening crops of all kinds.

The Banks of Newfoundland.—The Banks of Newfoundland are the most remarkable submarine elevations in the world. They are at some distance from the shores of the island, the nearest being less than 100 miles distant. It was once supposed that they had been formed by masses of sand and rock, borne thither by the river St. Lawrence, the Gulf Stream, and the Arctic current. It is now known that they are immense rocky elevations, forming submarine plateaus, whose eastern and southern borders descend steeply to a great depth. The Great Bank extends over fully 9 degrees of latitude from north to south; from east to west it covers in some places 5 degrees. The depth of water on the Bank varies from 50 to 360 feet. Beyond the Grand Bank to the eastward lies the Outer or False Bank, upon which the sea is from 600 to 900 feet in depth. To the west there are several smaller banks. At the west end of the Great Bank soundings have shown a depth of 9,000 feet. The depth around the Bank is from 10,000 to 15,000 feet. The fishing-grounds do not extend over the whole Bank, but have an extent of about 200 miles in length and 67 in breadth. For nearly 400 years this "cod-meadow" has been fished by large fleets of various nations, without showing any decrease in productiveness.

The cod taken on the Banks are larger and finer in quality than the fish taken on the shores of the island or on Labrador. They are known as "Bank-fish." An average of thirty Bank cod, when dried, will make a quintal. They bring a higher price than shore fish. The prevalent opinion is that the Bank cod are a different species from those taken on the shore. The eminent Swedish naturalist, Sars, has recently proved by his researches that this is a mistake, and that the shore and Bank cod are really the same species. The Bank cod are merely the mature, full-grown cod that have reached their fourth year or upwards; their habits at that age leading them to prefer the Banks to the shore as feeding-grounds. The two-year old and three-year old cod remain on the shore all the year, passing to and from the shallower water. When four years old their reproductive instincts are developed; and after spawning they retire far from the coast, and are found on the submarine slopes and valleys of the Great Banks. On the Labrador coast and on Finmark, in Norway, great numbers of small cod are taken, from 18 to 22 inches in length; and these are probably schools in their second or third year, which in a season or two, when mature, will change their mode of existence and become Bank fish.

The cod begin to appear each year, on the coast of Newfoundland, about the 1st of June, and are preceded by enormous schools of caplin, on which they feed. On the coast of the island the fishing-season lasts about 143 days; on Southern Labrador, 87 days; on Northern Labrador, 52 days. In October the cod begin to retire to their winter feeding-grounds in deep water, where they remain till the following June. Their migrations are thus from the deep water to the shallower water near the shore, which, being warmer in summer, is favourable for spawning. Each colony of cod appears to have its own winter feeding-ground, in deep water, at no great distance from the coast, and passes thence to its summer-feeding and spawning-grounds by the shortest route. It is a peculiarity of the cod, and of all fish, that they return to the locality where they were spawned to "repeat the story of their birth" by a continuation of the species. Hence the same varieties of cod are found on the same fishing-grounds year after year, and are easily distinguishable, one from the other; those taken at the north of the island, for example, being different from the southern varieties.

CHRONOLOGICAL SUMMARY. — CHAPTER XIII.

A.D.
1815. Commercial disasters in Newfoundland.
1816. Admiral Pickmore, first resident governor in Newfoundland.
1816–17. Three great Fires in St. John's, N.F.
1817. Death of the Princess Charlotte.
1819. The Atlantic first crossed by Steam.
1820. George IV. began to reign.
1821. Death of Napoleon Bonaparte, at St. Helena.
1824. Supreme Court reorganized in Newfoundland.
1825. Louis XVIII. died.
First roads made in Newfoundland.
1827. Battle of Navarino.
1829. Catholic Emancipation granted.
1830. William IV. began to reign.
First Railway opened between Liverpool and Manchester.
Charles X., of France, dethroned.
1831. First Appearance of Cholera in England.
1832. First Reform Act passed in England.
Representative Government granted to Newfoundland.
1833. Slavery abolished by England.
1837. Queen Victoria began to reign.
The Papineau and McKenzie Rebellion in Canada.
1839. Penny postage in England.
First Afghan War.
1840. Marriage of Queen Victoria and Prince Albert.
The two Canadas united.
1842. The Ashburton Treaty between England and the United States.
1842–49. "Amalgamated Assembly" in Newfoundland.

1845. Famine in Ireland.
1846. Great Fire in St. John's, N.F.
Repeal of the Corn Laws.
1847. Responsible Government granted to Canada.
1848. Responsible Government granted to Nova Scotia and New Brunswick.
Third French Revolution — Louis Philippe dethroned.
1851. First Submarine Cables between England and France.
First Great Exhibition in London.
Responsible Government granted to Prince Edward Island.
1852. Submarine Cable between England and Ireland.
1853. North-west Passage discovered by McClure.
1854. Responsible Government granted to Newfoundland.
Reciprocity Treaty between United States and British Provinces.
Russian War — Battles of Alma, Balaklava, and Inkerman.
1855. Fall of Sebastopol.
Death of Czar Nicholas.
1857. Mutiny in India — Massacre of Cawnpore — Sieges of Lucknow and Delhi.
1858. Great Eastern Steamship launched.
First Atlantic Cable laid.
1861. American Civil War commenced — ended 1865.
Death of Prince Albert.

CHAPTER XIV.

FROM 1861 TO 1884.

IMPORTANT EVENTS.

FAILURE OF THE FISHERIES. — DESTITUTION AND SUFFERING. — EVILS OF PAUPER RELIEF. — FIRST MINE OPENED. — GEOLOGICAL SURVEY. — OCEANIC AND COASTAL STEAM SERVICES. — IMPROVEMENT IN THE FISHERIES. — FIRST RAILWAY. — DRY DOCK OPENED.

1. It now remains briefly to narrate the most important events in the history of the colony during the last twenty-four years. The first nine years of that period were marked by unproductive fisheries, which caused widespread destitution and much suffering among the people. Since 1855 a practice had grown up of distributing, out of the public funds, relief to those who were in want during the winter season. This dangerous system of giving pauper-relief to able-bodied persons soon produced most injurious results. Many speedily learned to rely on this relief, and to look for it as a right each winter season. In consequence they became indolent and reckless, and made little effort to provide for themselves by honest labour and economy. So numerous became the applicants for relief that at length they ceased to feel any shame at being placed on the pauper-list. Ere long nearly a third of the entire revenue was required for the relief of the destitute. The evil had reached such dimensions that the government found great difficulty in dealing with it, especially when repeated failures of the fisheries had impoverished large

numbers of the fishermen, who had no other means of subsistence.

2. Sir Alexander Bannerman, the Governor, when opening the legislative session in 1860, referred to this condition of the working-classes, and urged that " no pains should be spared to give encouragement to agriculture, and to every other source that can give employment to the labouring classes, to prevent as far as possible their resorting to pauper relief." The revenue of 1861 fell to £81,000, and the public debt, which had been mainly incurred in meeting the necessities of the destitute, now amounted to £180,000. The Governor's speech, in 1863, again announced " wide-spread pauperism," in consequence of the failure of the previous year's fisheries. In 1864 Mr. Anthony Musgrave was appointed Governor. He had to repeat the same sad tale for four successive years, in addressing the legislators. No improvement in the fisheries took place, want among the people deepened and extended, and the financial condition of the country became worse and worse. During this period of depression large numbers of the people emigrated to the United States and Canada, despairing of their prospects in the colony.

3. The cause of these sufferings was very easily discovered. The great bulk of the people were entirely dependent on the precarious fisheries, and, when these gave poor returns, they had no other resource on which they could fall back. The population had been steadily increasing. The census of 1857 gave the total population of the island as 124,288. The census of 1869 showed that the population had increased to 146,536. Meantime the products of the fisheries had fallen off, and it became evident that a rapidly increasing population could no longer be sustained by a single industry. The

BETT'S COVE HARBOUR, NOTRE DAME BAY.

plain remedy lay in opening up other sources of employment for the people. The soil and climate were well adapted to the requirements of the farmer; but the old restrictive system had repressed agriculture in former periods, and the want of roads still rendered it impossible to settle the fertile valleys of the interior. With rich natural resources all around, large numbers of the people were sinking into destitution and misery. To all discerning minds it became clear that the remedy lay in promoting the cultivation of the soil, and encouraging other industries of a local kind, in which the surplus population might find remunerative employment.

4. It was at this dark period in the history of the colony that a most important discovery was made, which aided largely in bringing about an improved condition of affairs, and in diffusing new spirit and energy among the people. This was the discovery of valuable mineral deposits on the shores of Notre Dame Bay, leading to the introduction of mining enterprises. The first copper-mine was opened at Tilt Cove, in the year 1864. The honour of being the pioneer in mining belongs to Mr. C. F. Bennett, who for a length of time was almost alone in prosecuting the search for minerals in the island. The honour of being the actual discoverer of the first copper-mine belongs to Mr. Smith Mackay. In 1857, when exploring in the northern part of the island, Mr. Mackay found what proved to be a large deposit of copper ore, at a little fishing hamlet called Tilt Cove. It was not worked effectually by Messrs. Bennett and Mackay, the proprietors, till 1864. At the close of 1879 this mine had yielded neary 52,000 tons of ore, valued at more than a million and a half of dollars. In 1875 another copper-mine was opened at Bett's Cove, which, at the end of 1879, had yielded

125,556 tons of ore, valued at $2,982,836. The total quantity of ore exported up to the close of 1879 was valued at $4,629,899, or nearly £1,000,000 sterling. A third mine was opened at Little Bay, in 1878, which proved to be more valuable than either of the others. Various other mines have been worked with more or less success, and mining is now an established industry in the island, which ranks sixth among the copper-producing countries of the world. It is now known that there are in Newfoundland over 5,000 square miles of mineral lands, in which there can be little doubt rich discoveries await future explorers.

5. The beneficial effects of this new industry were speedily felt. Hundreds received remunerative employment at the mines. Capital was attracted to the country. Large amounts of money were distributed as wages. The working-classes were better provided with the necessaries and comforts of life. A more hopeful and enterprising spirit was awakened; and greater confidence in the future of the colony began to be felt.

6. These hopeful views regarding the natural capabilities of the country were greatly strengthened and extended by the results of the geological survey of the island, which was commenced, under the auspices of the government, in 1864. This survey was conducted by Mr. Alexander Murray, assisted latterly by Mr. James P. Howley. The work was prosecuted for eighteen years. For the first time the natural resources of the country were examined and reported on by well-qualified, scientific men. People learned from the reports of this survey, published yearly, and on authority that could not be questioned, that the interior of Newfoundland contains many fertile valleys, in which thousands of industrious settlers may find homes; extensive forests

of great value; beds of coal, marble, and gypsum; and mineral tracts which the labours of many generations are not likely to exhaust. Messrs. Murray and Howley's reports showed that there are nearly three millions of acres more or less adapted for settlement, and immense tracts fitted for raising sheep and cattle. It is now placed beyond all doubt that the island presents a promising field for mining enterprises, and contains enough of fertile land to sustain a large population in comfort.

7. The year 1869 brought a favourable turn in the tide of affairs, in the shape of abundant fisheries,— the first for nine years which could be called generally successful. Many of the people had been devoting themselves more to the cultivation of the land, and the harvest of this year was good. The improvement in the fisheries in 1869 proved to be the commencement of a series of productive fisheries, which continued up to the summer of 1884, when a decline took place. This increase was accompanied by an advance in the price of the cod-fishery products in foreign markets. The sun of prosperity once more began to shine. The wonderful elasticity of the business of the country was shown in its rapid recovery from depression. Harvests proved to be fairly good. The revenue derived from duties on importations increased as the people were able to purchase more freely the necessaries and comforts of life. In 1871 the revenue amounted to £207,790,— the largest ever received. The new industry of mining advanced rapidly. The improved condition of the revenue permitted increased grants to be made for the construction of roads, bridges, wharves, light-houses, and other works of public utility.

8. A general election took place towards the close of 1869, when Sir Stephen Hill was Governor. The impor-

tant question was then submitted to the electors, whether steps should be taken to unite the colony with the newly formed Dominion of Canada, so as to constitute one of its provinces. The results of the election showed that a large majority of the people were opposed to confederation with Canada. So strongly did public feeling show itself that the question of union with the Dominion has ever since been entirely laid aside.

9. In 1873 direct steam communication with England and America was established. The arrangement entered into with the Montreal Steamship Company, for the conveyance of mails, passengers, and goods, secured fortnightly calls of homeward and outward bound ships of the Allan Line, at St. John's, during nine months of the year, and monthly trips, *via* Halifax, during the remainder. The latter have recently become fortnightly trips also. The trade and commerce of the country were greatly benefited by this improved means of communication with the outside world. Local steam communication between St. John's and the most important towns and settlements north and south was also improved and extended. The interests of education were not forgotten. The legislative grant for the support of schools and academies was increased to $93,952 per annum. In 1881 there were in the island 416 elementary schools, attended by 24,292 pupils, and 674 pupils attending the academies; while there were 84 pupil teachers under training, to take charge of schools. In St. John's, factories of various kinds began to spring up, affording increased employment to considerable numbers. These have proved so successful that every year witnesses an increase of their number.

10. These were all substantial and cheering improvements, indicating an advance of the colony in all the great essentials of civilization. But the greatest stride in progress still remained to be taken. While in all the neighbouring colonies extensive lines of railway had been constructed and worked most advantageously, in Newfoundland not a mile of railway had yet been built. Now, however, when a knowledge of the great natural resources of the country had been diffused, and when the necessity of providing new means of employment for the increasing population had secured the attention of thoughtful men, the construction of a railway, to open up the country to industrial enterprise, began to be discussed. At first many objections were raised, and many shrank from the proposal, believing a railway to be unnecessary, and beyond the means of the colony. New projects of this kind are sure to encounter more or less opposition. The question, however, still pressed for solution: "What are we to do in the future, with our ever-increasing population, who cannot find sustenance from the employment furnished by the fisheries? Here are fertile lands and great forests. How are we to bring together the idle hands and the unoccupied lands?" The project of a railway continued to grow in public favour, and, at length, in 1875, the Legislature voted a sum of money for a preliminary survey of a line from St. John's to St. George's Bay, which was carried out the same year. It was afterwards found that the British Government could not be induced to sanction the construction of this line, as its terminus would be on the so-called " French Shore," regarding which negotiations with France were then in progress. The matter, therefore, had to be laid aside for a time.

11. In the summer of 1876 the Fishery Commission, in connection with the Treaty of Washington, met in Halifax. The Hon. W. V. Whiteway was the delegate

from Newfoundland. The Commission awarded five and a half millions of dollars as compensation for fisheries' rights extended to the United States by the British Provinces. Of this sum Newfoundland received one million dollars.

12. Sir John Hawley Glover was appointed Governor in 1876. He proved himself to be possessed of enlightened and progressive views, and energetically urged forward public improvements. In order to acquaint himself with the condition of the country and the wants of the people he made repeated voyages to different places around the coast. In the autumn of 1878 he made a journey across the island from Hall's Bay to Bay of Islands. In opening the Legislature, the following year, he said: " My visit forcibly impressed me with the rich agricultural resources of this portion of the island, and the value of the forest lands, — provisions of nature destined soon to attract and reward large numbers of industrious settlers."

13. During the legislative session of 1880 decisive steps were taken towards the construction of a railway. Sir W. V. Whiteway, premier, moved that the colony should, out of its own revenues, construct a railway of about 340 miles in length, from St. John's to Hall's Bay, in the mining district, having branches to Harbour Grace, Brigus, and other centres of population. Such a line, he showed, would open up the fertile lands in the valleys of the Gambo, Gander, and Exploits, and would connect the mining region and various populous districts with the capital. The question was referred to a joint-committee composed of members of both branches of the Legislature. Their report was highly favourable to the construction of this line of railway, and recommended that £1,000,000 sterling should be borrowed on the credit of the colony, and the work at once commenced. In the following year, 1881, the Legislature entered into a contract with " the Newfoundland Railway Company " for the construction and operation of this line, for which they agreed to give the company an annual subsidy, and also grants of land on each side of the railway. On the 9th of August, 1881, the first sod of

GOVERNMENT HOUSE.

the railway was turned. The event marks an important epoch in the history of the colony. In December, 1884. the first 86 miles of the line were completed and opened for traffic, between St. John's and Harbour Grace, — the second town in the island. Large sums of money were paid to the labouring-class who were employed on the work, while the trading-classes also shared in the benefits.

14. In 1881 Sir Henry Fitzhardinge Maxse was appointed Governor. At the opening of the Legislature, in 1882, Sir F. B. Carter, who acted as administrator of the government, in the absence of the Governor, caused by ill-

NOTES AND EXPLANATIONS.—CHAPTER XIV.

St. John's Water-Works.—The terrible devastations wrought by fire in the capital at length taught the people the necessity of introducing such a supply of water as would prove a safeguard against the destroyer. After the great fire of 1846 the city was rebuilt on an improved plan, the streets were widened, and fire-breaks provided. Wooden buildings in the business part of the city were prohibited. It was not, however, till 1860 that the present abundant supply of excellent water was secured. The water is conducted in pipes from Windsor Lake, five miles distant from St. John's, and situated at a height above it of 500 feet. The pressure is thus so great that there is no need of engines, as water from the hydrants can be thrown over the highest buildings. The supply of water is abundant, and the consumption unrestricted. Three millions of gallons are run off daily in the city. The water is soft, pure, and excellent for all household purposes. There are efficient volunteer fire-brigades. No fire of any considerable extent has occurred since the introduction of the water, and few cities enjoy greater security against fire, notwithstanding that two-thirds of it consist of wooden houses.

The water-works were constructed by a joint-stock company, with a capital of $400,000, the interest on which is guaranteed by government at the rate of five per cent., and paid by a rate levied on the consumers. The importance of such a supply of water cannot be overrated, as it has greatly improved the public health, and promoted habits of cleanliness among the working-classes, as well as provided a security against fires. The reduction in the rates of fire insurance since the new supply of water covers the water-rates.

History of the Seal-Fishery.—While the cod-fishery has been prosecuted for nearly 400 years, the seal-fishery is not more than 80 years old, and may be said to date from 1805. Hackluyt, the historian of the early voyagers, tells us that " in 1593 there were on the shores of the island of Ramea, within the Straits of St. Peter, on the back of Newfoundland, chiefly in April, May, and June, multitudes of amphibious creatures called *vaccæ marinæ*, or morses, the two large teeth of which, resembling ivory, and their oil were considered as valuable articles of commerce; that Captain Drake found there a ship belonging to the inhabitants of St. Malo, almost full-freighted with morses; that he also observed several whales of an enormous size, together with great numbers of seals and porpoises, of which they killed several." Up to 1774 this fishery referred to by Hackluyt was prosecuted around the island. The " sea-cow or morse " of those days was the walrus, and was valuable for its oil, skin, and tusks, the latter furnishing the best ivory. These tusks, two in number, hang from the upper jaw, and by them the walrus lifts itself on the ice. Gradually the animal became extinct in those seas, and is now confined to the Arctic regions. A whale-fishery was carried on from 1760 for a number of years in the gulf and river of St. Lawrence, to which the New England people at one time sent from 50 to 80 vessels annually. A few whales are still taken in Fortune Bay, but the fishery is now unimportant.

The first mention of a seal-fishery is by L'Abbe Raynal, who tells us, that, as early as 1763, some English fishermen used to repair to certain parts of the coast of Newfoundland, during winter, for the prosecution of the seal-fishery. This was an inshore net-fishery, and was carried on upon a small scale, and is still followed along shore, in some favourable localities. The fishermen place their nets between the shore and the islands or rocks lying at a short distance from it, and the seals, in passing these narrow places, are caught.

The next step in the seal-fishery was the shooting of seals from large boats, which left port about the middle of April. As late as 1795 the whole catch of seals was under 5,000. Soon after, the sealing-boats gave place to small schooners of thirty to fifty tons, carrying twelve to fourteen men each, and not leaving port till after March 21st. Conception Bay led the way in this new industry, and its people showed much energy, and many of them became wealthy in the prosecution of the seal-fishery. In 1807 about fifty of these small schooners were engaged in seal-hunting from various ports. It proved so remunerative that its growth was rapid. In 1805, 81,088 seals were taken; in 1815, 126,315; in 1820, 213,679; in 1830, 558,942; in 1840, 631,385; in 1844, 685,530 seals, the largest number ever taken in one year. In 1857 there were nearly 400 vessels, of from 80 to 200 tons, engaged in the seal-fishery, their united crews numbering 13,600 men, the total catch of that year being close on half a million seals, worth $1,700,000. The catch of seals has not increased since that date, and occasionally it has fallen low, as in 1882, when only 200,500 seals were taken, and in 1884, when 238,587 were taken.

In 1863 the first steamer took part in this fishery. Since then the number of steamers has rapidly increased, and the number of sailing vessels has steadily diminished. The same work is now done by fewer hands, so that fewer men find employment in this industry. It is not unlikely that in a few more years this fishery will be entirely carried on by powerful steamers. In competition with steamers, sailing-vessels have but a poor chance of success. About 8,000 to 9,000 men are now engaged in it. Sailing-vessels are permitted to leave port for the ice-fields on the 1st of March; steamers cannot leave till the 10th of March. In 1881 there were 24 steamers employed, but their number has since been reduced. Seven of those sealing-steamers come from Dundee, Scotland, each spring, and take their crew in Newfoundland. When the seal-fishery terminates, these steamers proceed to the Arctic whale-fishery, returning to Dundee in October.

The Islands of St. Pierre and Miquelon. — These little islands, at the mouth of Fortune Bay, as we have learned in the course of this history, were ceded by Great Britain to France as a shelter for her fishermen. They are thus the only existing relics of the once great French empire in America, which stretched from Hudson's Bay to the mouths of the Mississippi, comprising the present British possessions in North America and the great valley of the Mississippi, — or about one-half of the North American continent. The *fleur-de-lis* had to withdraw from these regions one after the other, and now it only waves over these insignificant rocky islets. The British Lion has taken all, and left to France only the privilege of fishing on a portion of the coast of Newfoundland, with St. Pierre and Miquelon for a shelter.

To France these islands are of great value. Under the shadow of the tri-colour lives here a little world of fishermen, who, amid the perils of a stormy sea, ply their avocation. From the encompassing waters France derives an important part of her food supply. To their ports Spain sends yearly enormous quantities of salt, for preserving the precious gifts of the sea, which are found here in inexhaustible abundance. Thousands of French fishermen repair to these bleak islets, not only to gather the sea-harvest, but to train themselves, by battling with the billows, for service in the navy of their country.

The group of islets consists of St. Pierre, Grande-Miquelon, and Petite-Miquelon or Langlade. The resident population now amounts to 5,000. Since 1783 the Grande and Petite-Miquelon have been united by a sand-bank. They are distant 135 miles from Cape Ray and Cape Race, the south-western and south-eastern extremities of Newfoundland. Great Miquelon is not more than three-fourths of a league in length. St. Pierre is much smaller, but contains the capital of the same name, and is three times more populous than the former. The Governor of the whole group resides at St. Pierre. The town is surrounded by low hills. In the fishing season it presents quite an animated appearance, being crowded with the floating population from France, which greatly exceeds the resident inhabitants. Vegetation on the islands is of the poorest description, only a few garden vegetables being grown. The climate resembles that of the ports on the Gulf of St. Lawrence. Dense fogs prevail in summer, and often hang over them for days in succession. St. Pierre is the only good harbour. Fifty or sixty fishing vessels are often seen lying securely in its waters. The other harbours are unsafe when certain winds blow.

More than three-fourths of all the codfish consumed in France come from St. Pierre and Miquelon. Official returns show that during the five years, ending in 1871, the catch of cod here averaged 15,423,086 kilograms. The same returns show that, for the five years ending in 1874, the average number of vessels employed was 76; of boats, 590; the total tonnage of which was 12,386; and the number of men employed, 5,335.

In 1868 a French Cable Company was formed to lay a submarine cable between Brest and St. Pierre, and from the latter island to Duxbury, Massachusetts. This cable was successfully laid in 1869, three years after the successful establishment of telegraphic communication between Heart's Content, Newfoundland, and the British Isles, in 1866. Previously, in 1858, a cable had been laid over the same route, between Ireland and Newfoundland, but worked only for a short time.

CHRONOLOGICAL SUMMARY. — CHAPTER XIV.

A.D.
- 1863. Prince of Wales married.
- 1864. Canadian Confederation carried in Quebec Conference.
  First copper-mine opened in Newfoundland.
  Geological survey commenced in Newfoundland.
- 1865. President Lincoln assassinated.
- 1866. Dominion of Canada proclaimed. — Intercolonial Railway authorized.
- 1867. Second Reform Act in England. — Household suffrage in boroughs.
- 1869. Irish Church disestablished.
  Newfoundland rejected confederation with Canada.
- 1871. Treaty of Washington.
  British Columbia entered the Dominion.
- 1872. Vote by ballot in England.
- 1873. Prince Edward Island entered the Dominion.
- 1874. Ashantee War.
- 1875. First government railway survey in Newfoundland.
- 1876. Fishery Commission met in Halifax.
- 1877. Russo-Turkish War.
- 1878. Treaty of Berlin.
  Second Afghan War.
  Zulu War.
- 1881. Second Irish Land Act.
  First sod of Newfoundland Railway turned Aug. 9th.
- 1883. Dry-dock, St. John's, N.F., commenced.
- 1884. Third Reform Act in England. — Household suffrage in counties. Redistribution of seats.
  Railway to Harbour Grace opened.
  Dry-dock, St. John's, opened.

CHAPTER XV.

CONCLUSION.

RETROSPECT AND PROSPECT. — PROGRESS OF THE COLONY. — IMPROVEMENTS IN ST. JOHN'S. — GENERAL PROSPERITY OF THE PEOPLE. — A GREAT FUTURE IN STORE FOR NEWFOUNDLAND.

1. We have now bought the history of the oldest British colony down to the latest date. We have seen the vicissitudes and trials through which it has passed; the misgovernment which so long retarded its prosperity; the adversities from which it ever rose triumphant. In battling with their difficulties we have seen how its people gained in energy, courage, and intelligence, and won their freedom by their activity and patient endurance. A brighter and happier future now opens before them and their children. Their country is advancing in importance and strength, — in all that constitutes the essentials of well-being for a free people. They now regard it as a home for themselves and their posterity, which, by industry and wise guidance, may be beautified and developed into greatness, and made a country which will occupy a proud position among surrounding communities.

2. That Newfoundland has recently made great and substantial progress, especially during the last twelve years, cannot be denied by any one acquainted with its condition. A glance at its capital furnishes abundant proof of this. The town of St. John's, which, at the beginning of this century, was a small collection of mean, wooden houses, huddled into a narrow space around the harbour, without any sanitary arrangements, and continually subject to devastations by fire, has grown into a well-built, prosperous city, of more than 30,000 inhabi-

CHURCH OF ENGLAND CATHEDRAL, ST. JOHN'S.

tants. It possesses two stately cathedrals, handsome churches, creditable public halls, an athenæum building, banks, stores of all kinds, mercantile premises, and shops of imposing dimensions, commodious and well-built houses, extensive wharves. Every year witnesses the erection of new and better houses for the accommodation of the increasing population. Its factories of various kinds, its iron foundries and machine-shops, give employment to large numbers, and testify to the healthy growth of native industries. Its supply of excellent water is abundant. Its harbour can boast of what is believed to be the largest dry dock in the world. A railway has been commenced, which, in the course of years, will connect it with all the centres of population throughout the island. A busy, thriving population throng its streets. Its trade is very large. Lectures, concerts, and social entertainments of all kinds show that its people are advancing in culture and education. Its charitable and benevolent institutions and societies furnish ample proof that the poor are cared for. Numerous schools and academies show that the interests of education are not overlooked. Many improvements have yet to be introduced; many reforms are needed; but that genuine and striking progress has been made every one must allow. This is a guarantee of greater progress in the future.

3. Other towns throughout the island are sharing, more or less, in the spirit of progress; and, as they are more brought into connection with the capital, civilizing influences will be more felt. Harbour Grace is a handsome town of nearly 8,000 inhabitants; the streets are wide and well laid out. It is lighted with gas, and has an excellent system of water-works. Carbonear has also obtained an abundant supply of good water; and will soon be reached by the railway. In Placentia, Trinity, Bonavista, Catalina, Twillingate, improvements are steadily making way.

4. Turning to the general condition of the colony we

CONCLUSION. 167

see on all hands evidences of progress. The revenue has more than doubled within the last twenty years, and now reaches nearly a million and a quarter dollars annually. As it is derived mainly from duties on importations, the increase of revenue shows an improvement in the condition of the people and in their means of pur-

ROMAN CATHOLIC CATHEDRAL, ST. JOHN'S.

chasing the necessaries and luxuries of life. Taxation is less than in any other British colony. In 1883 the total value of imports was $9,131,464; of exports, $7,996,-795. In 1870 the value of exports was $6,984,543; of imports, $6,655,849. The increase in thirteen years is significant. In 1884 the value of the exports was $9,061,186. On December 31, 1883, the registered tonnage of the colony was 1,988 vessels, of which 27 were steamers, having a tonnage of 91,767 tons. In the same year 55 new vessels were built in the country, their tonnage being 2,330 tons. At the beginning of this century the whole population was 20,000; now it has reached 197,589.

5. That the cod-fishery, the staple industry of the country, is not declining is evident from the fact that, in 1883-84 no less than 1,733,417 quintals of dried codfish were exported, so that the catch in 1883 was the largest on record. In that year the volume of trade (imports and exports combined) was in value $17,128,259, — an amount not reached in any previous year. Roadmaking has been carried on since 1825, and now over $100,000 annually are spent in making and repairing roads and bridges. There are at present about 727 miles of postal roads, and 1,730 miles of district roads, while many more miles are in course of construction. The fine steamers of the Allan Line make weekly calls at St. John's, and afford speedy means of communication with Britain and America. Local steamers connect the principal outports with the capital. All these indicate an increase in wealth and in the appliances of civilized life.

6. As yet only the fringe around the coast of the island is occupied. The fertile lands, the great forests of the interior, are still untouched. The mineral treasures are barely opened; the coal-beds are yet undisturbed. When these are turned to account the population of the island will be reckoned by millions. Sooner or later this great island is destined to be overspread by a thriving, industrious population who will utilize its splendid resources.

7. Thus facts warrant us in predicting a great future for Newfoundland. In its treasures of sea and land, of

forest and mine, Nature has bestowed on its people a noble heritage. The riches of its encompassing seas are

COCHRANE-STREET METHODIST CHURCH, ST. JOHN'S.

inexhaustible, — "greater than the gold and silver mines of Mexico and Peru." Three centuries have failed to show any diminution in their value, though ever-increasing drafts have been made on those treasures of the deep. The Great Banks, 600 miles in length, with their swarming fish-life, are but a day's sail from the shores of the island. In its dependency of Labrador the colony has another fishing-ground of incalculable value. In the summer of 1883 there were taken on Labrador 650,000 quintals of codfish, and the total value of its produce that year was $2,592,000. The seal-fishery, prosecuted at a time when no other marine industries are practicable, yields an average of a million and a quarter of dollars annually. The geographical position of the island for commercial purposes could not be surpassed; it is but 1,640 miles from the coast of Ireland; it commands the entrance to the Gulf of St. Lawrence; its noble bays stretch their arms inland from 50 to 100 miles; its harbours are among the finest in the world. Before many years have passed, a steam-ferry will connect it with the eastern terminus of the Canadian system of railways. Among the wonders in store for the future it is not impossible that the shortest and safest travel-route between the Old and New World should yet be found across the Island of Newfoundland.

8. The present population of Newfoundland has sprung from two of the greatest and most energetic races of the world,— the Saxon and Celtic. In the healthy, invigorating climate of the island the blood has not deteriorated. Its climate is admirably fitted to nurture a people of great physical power and mental energy, who will be able to hold a distinguished place among the English-speaking communities of the New World. To this end they should take care that their educational system shall keep pace with their material prosperity; that no child shall be allowed to grow up in ignorance; and that due provision be made for the higher education which is needed to promote the intellectual life of the

people. Many of the troubles of the past have arisen from differences in race and religion among the people. Thence have come, at times, jealousies, antipathies, and

ST. ANDREW'S PRESBYTERIAN CHURCH, ST. JOHN'S.

injurious contentions. In the better spirit which now prevails these will gradually disappear. The distinctions of English, Scotch, and Irish, Protestants and Catholics, will merge into the common name of Newfoundlanders, which all will be proud to bear; and the love of a common country will obliterate the differences

ROMAN CATHOLIC CATHEDRAL, HARBOUR GRACE.

and rivalries of the past. Then the great rivalry will be as to who can turn to the best advantage the gifts of Providence, and most effectually advance the best interests of a free, united, and happy people.

QUESTIONS FOR EXAMINATION ON CHAPTER XV.

1. What of the better future now opening for Newfoundland?

2. Give proofs of recent progress in the capital. Enumerate the public buildings. What shows social advance?

3. What improvements have been made in other towns?

4. What proofs of progress does the condition of the colony show? Give the value of imports and exports in 1870 and in 1883. What was the value of exports in 1884? Give particulars of the shipping.

5. How many quintals of codfish were exported in 1883–84? What of roads?

6. What are the prospects of settling the interior?

7. Why may we believe in a great future for Newfoundland? Show the value of the Labrador fisheries, and of the seal-fishery. Show the advantages of the geographical position of the island. Why is it likely to be the shortest travel-route between Europe and America? What of the people and their future? What has been the cause of social disturbances in the past? How are these to be avoided in the future?

NOTES AND EXPLANATIONS.—CHAPTER XV.

The People of Newfoundland—Their Physique.—Newfoundlanders are, in their general physique, a powerfully built, robust, and hardy race. They and their fathers have buffeted the billows, fought the terrible ice-floes, and drunk in the health-giving sea-breezes Engaged largely in open-air occupations, and breathing an invigorating atmosphere, a strong, energetic race has grown up, who are well-fitted for the world's rough work. From the hardy, much-enduring race who have been developed here, often fighting cold and hunger, drawing their scanty subsistence mainly from the boisterous seas, fearlessly pursuing their avocations amid storms and ice-fields, will spring a people who, when duly educated and cultured, may be expected to play a worthy part in the world of the future. The noblest nations of the earth, past and present, were not nurtured amid the flowers of the south, but in the cold and stern north, where nature had to be conquered by labour and sweat of brow, and where the barren wilderness had to be transformed by hard toil into the waving cornfield. Kingsley, in his "Ode to the North-East Wind," says:—

> Let the luscious south-wind
>   Breathe in lovers' sighs,
> While the lazy gallants
>   Bask in ladies' eyes.
> What does he but soften
>   Heart alike and pen?
> *'Tis the hard, gray weather*
>   *Breeds hard Englishmen.*
>
> What's the soft south-wester?
>   'Tis the ladies' breeze,
> Bringing home their true loves
>   Out of all the seas;
> But the black north-easter,
>   Through the snow-storm hurled,
> Drives our English hearts of oak
>   Seaward round the world!
>
> Come as came our fathers,
>   Heralded by thee,
> Conquering from the eastward,
>   Lords by land and sea.
> Come, and strong within us
>   Stir the Vikings' blood,
> Bracing brain and sinew,—
>   Blow, thou wind of God!

Names of Places. — The changes in names of places are curious, and sometimes difficult to trace. Carbonear was formerly written Carboneir, and was originally Carboniero (Spanish or Portuguese evidently). Torbay, in old books, is Thorne-Bay. Bay of Bulls is said originally to have been Baboul Bay; others make it a corruption of the French *Baie de Boules*. Trepassey Bay, Anspach says, was formerly *Abram Trepassé*. Fermuse was anciently Fermose or Fermosa, — beautiful. Renewes, formerly Renowes, or Reneau's Harbour. La Poile, so named by the French from its supposed resemblance to a frying-pan. Great Burgeo Island is also called Eclipse Island, from the fact that Captain Cook observed an eclipse of the sun there in 1765. Point Enragée, so named from its exposed situation. Cape Spear, near St. John's, was originally Cape Espere or Espoir, or Cape Hope. Great Bruit, great noise; Rose Blanche, white rose; Bay-of-Cinq-Cerfs, or Five Stags, explain their own origin. The small river which falls into the head of St. John's Harbour was once called Little Castor's River, a name not heard now.

Richard Hakluyt, whose narratives of early voyages and discoveries are so valuable, and so often quoted, was a clergyman of the Church of England, and at one time prebendary of the cathedral of Bristol. He was born in 1553, and studied at Christ Church, Oxford. He made a special study of geography, or cosmography, as it was then called, and was made a lecturer on this subject at Oxford. He took an active part in encouraging and directing the spirit of discovery in those days. He was associated with Sir Walter Raleigh in his effort at planting Virginia. In 1589 he published his "Collection of Travels," in one volume, folio, which he afterwards enlarged and published in three volumes, folio, under the title, "The Principal Navigations and Discoveries of the English Nation, by sea or overland to the remote and farthest distant quarters of the earth, at any time within the compass of these 1500 years." Hakluyt also published or edited translations of several foreign narratives of travellers, from which was published a "Selection of curious, rare, and early voyages, and histories of interesting discoveries, chiefly published by Hakluyt, or at his suggestion, but not included in his celebrated compilation: 4to, London, 1812." He died in 1616, and was buried in Westminster Abbey. His accounts of the early voyages to Newfoundland and the adjacent countries are of great value.

APPENDIX.

APPENDIX I.

EARLY HISTORY OF THE ATLANTIC CABLES.

THE story of the laying of the first Atlantic cables possesses a romantic interest; and, in connection with it, Newfoundland was destined to play an important part. On its shores the little cord which first bound together the Old World and the New found a resting-place, as it emerged from the depths of the ocean. From that moment the great crystal dome of the Atlantic became a whispering-gallery between two worlds. On the lightning's pinions thought flew between East and West. Modern civilization obtained a new birth. Humanity throbbed with a new life and a great hope. The English-speaking communities on opposite sides of the Atlantic, the leaders in the van of civilization, were united; and from that instantaneous inter-communication of thought what vast possibilities are opened up for the improvement and happiness of the race! Once more time and space were annihilated. "And I saw a great angel stand with one foot on the sea and another on the land; and he swore by Him that liveth, *that time shall be no more.*" The grand old prophecy has received a partial fulfilment.

Mr. Cyrus Field was the life and soul of the great enterprise; and to him, more than to any other man, the civilized world is indebted for its successful completion.

Others, no doubt, rendered important aid, and merit all honour. But his was the strong faith in the possibility of the work being done which never wavered amid disappointments and discouragements; and his the hope that he and his band of comrades should do it, which bore them triumphant over every failure. His fervid faith and buoyant hope proved contagious, and inspired even the cool calculators on the London and New York Stock Exchange, so that they were willing to drop million after million of dollars into the depths of the Atlantic on the bare chance of success. His inspiring hope lifted speculation into a higher and nobler atmosphere, and moved even cautious statesmen to render aid. For thirteen long years he clung to his great thought, like another Columbus, when others pronounced him a wild fanatic; and on the 5th of August, 1858, his wire touched the New World, and the first message was transmitted.

Previous to this, in 1854, the Legislature of Newfoundland had been the first to encourage Mr. Field and his friends, by granting them a most liberal charter in connection with the enterprise, which secured to them exclusive rights. Without this charter Mr. Field himself confessed that he could not have obtained the necessary money from capitalists. The first words in the Act which secured these privileges were as follows: "*Whereas* it is deemed advisable to establish a line of telegraphic communication between America and Europe by way of Newfoundland." The charter granted to his company the exclusive privilege of landing cables on the shores of Newfoundland for fifty years; but this was subject to the right of preëmption by the government at any time after twenty years.

The first step was to establish communication between Newfoundland and Cape Breton, by a cable across the Gulf of St. Lawrence, thence to Canada and the United States. When this was accomplished, the governments of Great Britain and the United States agreed to furnish ships to take soundings across the Atlantic and to assist in laying the cable. In the summer of 1857 the first attempt to lay the cable was made; but, after a few hundred miles were laid, it was lost. In the summer of 1858 the attempt was renewed. The cable was successfully landed on the 5th of August. It continued to work till the 1st of September; but, after four hundred messages had passed over it, the cable ceased to work. The enterprise at once fell into discredit, and its promoters were reckoned lunatics. Ten thousand dollars of the stock sold in New York for a ten-dollar greenback, and in London, a thousand pounds for thirty guineas. Few expected that the enterprise would ever be renewed. But Mr. Field never despaired; and, after unparalleled efforts, he succeeded in raising capital to make a new and better cable, which was loaded on board the "Great Eastern," in 1865. Once more disaster came. After twelve hundred miles of cable had been successfully payed out, the cable broke in water two miles in depth. With the greatest difficulty enough money was obtained to make a new cable, which was successfully laid, in 1866, and continued to work most satisfactorily. Not only so, but the end of the lost cable of 1865 was found and raised from a depth of two miles, and the laying triumphantly completed. Mr. Field was the hero of the hour. The world rejoiced over the completion of the great work.

Additional cables followed soon after. In 1871 another cable was laid along the same route; a fourth in 1873, and a fifth in 1880. The first cable of 1858, having been imperfectly constructed, has been abandoned; and at present there are five cables between Newfoundland and Ireland.

In 1869 the French Cable Company laid a cable from Brest to St. Pierre; thence to Duxbury, Massachusetts. The same company laid a second cable in 1879. In 1875 the Direct United States Cable Company laid a cable from Ireland to Torbay, in Nova Scotia; thence to Duxbury. In 1881 and 1882 two "American cables" were laid, and in 1884 the two Mackay-Bennett cables.

There is, however, one name seldom mentioned in connection with this great enterprise to which due honour has not been accorded. The man who pioneered the way for telegraphic communication across the Atlantic, and who was the practical prime-mover of the undertaking, was Mr. Frederick N. Gisborne, F.R.S.C, Engineer and Electrician, and at present Government Superintendent of the Telegraph and Signal Service of the Dominion of Canada. Mr. Gisborne is an Englishman, of an old Derbyshire family. In 1848 he was employed by the government of Nova Scotia in establishing telegraphic communication between Halifax, Canada, New Brunswick, and the United States. The late Hon. Joseph Howe, who at the time of his death was Lieutenant-Governor of Nova Scotia, has published a statement, dated February 12, 1867, in which he says, that in 1850 Mr. Gisborne laid before the Telegraph Commissioners in Halifax a plan for connecting Newfoundland with the continent of America by a submarine cable, and spoke confidently of being able to extend it across the Atlantic, and connect Europe with America. " Up to this time," says Mr. Howe, "I never heard the idea suggested; and, though reading the English and American papers, never saw an allusion to the practicability of such an enterprise." Now, if Mr. Gisborne had done nothing more than strike out this project, and if it had remained a mere thought in his mind, without producing fruit, he would be entitled to a comparatively slight meed of praise. The possibility or the probability of establishing electric communication across the Atlantic might occur to many minds, and vague suggestions to that effect might come from many quarters. Professor Morse, as early as 1843, from some of his experiments, wrote as follows to the Secretary of the United States: " The practical inference from this law is, that a telegraphic communication, on the electric-magnetic plan, may with certainty be established across the Atlantic ocean. Startling as this may seem now, I am confident the time will come when this project will be realized." A vast number of experiments and much toil of hand and brain were needed before this prophecy could be fulfilled, though the suggestion of such an eminent electrician as Professor Morse might set other minds working on the project. The true maker and inventor is not he who merely strikes out a thought, but who works out that thought into a practical result which the senses can appreciate, so that the vague idea takes form and substance and becomes a reality. Others may come after him, and vastly extend and improve his first imperfect attempt, and they deserve due recognition and praise; but the original inventor is he who produces the first tangible result.

Let us test Mr. Gisborne by this rule. He did not rest satisfied with striking out a plan, he proceeded to carry it into practical effect. He succeeded in interesting a number of capitalists of London and New York in the project, and formed "The New York and Newfoundland Telegraph Company," of which he was Superintendent and Engineer. He came to Newfoundland, and in 1852 the Legislature passed an act conferring the important privileges upon his company, in event of the completion of the project in Newfoundland, which the Atlantic Telegraph Company afterwards possessed. He went to work with energy, and commenced the construction of a telegraph line 400 miles in length, from St. John's to Cape Ray, over a most difficult country. In surveying and superintending this line he had to encounter the severest hardships, and to wrestle with innumerable difficulties. At great pecuniary sacrifice and risk of health he carried out the work. In 1852 he laid down a submarine cable between Prince Edward Island and New Brunswick, 11 miles in length, across the Straits of Northumberland. This was the first American submarine cable. Only one submarine cable was then in existence, namely, the cable between Dover and Calais, laid down by Brett, in 1851. It remained to lay down another cable between Cape Ray and Cape Breton. When that was done steamers then running between St. John's and Galway would shorten the time of receiving news between London and New York by four or five days. So much would be gained as a first step. Then would come Mr. Gisborne's greater stride of spanning the Atlantic by a cable, which he had propounded three years before.

But at this point, before he succeeded in laying the cable across the Gulf of St. Lawrence, misfortune overtook the great enterprise. Only a small amount of capital had been subscribed, and in 1853 the company became involved in pecuniary difficulties. Mr. Gisborne went to New York to endeavour to raise additional capital. Here accident brought him into communication with Mr. Cyrus W. Field, to whom he unfolded all his plans. At that time Mr. Field knew nothing of telegraphic matters, and had just returned from travelling in South America, with the intention of enjoying the fortune his industry and sagacity had secured ere he had arrived at the middle term of life. As he listened to Mr. Gisborne his keen, sagacious mind took in the whole grand enterprise, which seems at once to have fired his whole being. He had hardly slept till he was in communication with Professor Morse and Lieut. Maury, as to the possibility of laying down a wire and sending an electric current across the bed of the Atlantic. Their replies gave him increased confidence. He got several great capitalists to join him, such as Mr. Peter Cooper, Mr. Moses Taylor, Mr. Marshall O. Roberts, and Mr. Chandler White. They purchased from Mr. Gisborne the privileges of his company for £8,000. Mr. Field and others started for Newfoundland in the middle of March, 1854, and in April the Legislature passed the act already referred to, which gave his company the exclusive right of landing cables on the shores of the island for fifty years, subject to preëmption after twenty years. Then Mr. Field's great career commenced as the leader of the enterprise. Mr. Gisborne was appointed chief engineer of the new company.

We would not for a moment detract from the great services which Mr. Field thus rendered to the cause of civilization. His heroic perseverance in the face of difficulties that would have overwhelmed ordinary men; his unflinching confidence in the ultimate triumph of his enterprise; his self-sacrificing labours in connection with it; his penetrating, far-reaching insight into its importance to the world, — all these merit the highest admiration and praise. Mr. Field will be remembered as long as telegraphs unite the Old World and the New.

But while we give him his full meed of applause, let us not forget the far-seeing engineer, who not only struck out the idea at first, but took the first steps towards its practical realization, pioneered the way, and showed how it was to be done. Had it not been for the work he accomplished, and the length he attained towards success, Mr. Field and the great capitalists would hardly have been induced to venture their money in such an enterprise. With the name of Mr. Cyrus W. Field should be associated that of Mr. Frederick Newton Gisborne, the originator of the great enterprise.

Should any doubts be raised as to whether Mr. Gisborne entertained the larger project of spanning the Atlantic with a cable, the following extracts, which have been published from Mr. John Brett's letters to Mr. Gisborne, will settle the question in all candid minds. In 1853 Mr. Gisborne was in correspondence with Mr. Brett, the founder of submarine telegraphy in England, with the view of enlisting his coöperation in his project. Mr. Brett entertained his proposals most favourably; and, under date " London, July 8th, 1853," having previously received Mr. Gisborne's plans, he wrote as follows: " On my return from Paris I found your satisfactory letter of 4th June. Let me recommend you to secure in our joint names an exclusive privilege for establishing a submarine telegraph between Newfoundland and Ireland for fifty years."

It was when courageously preparing the way for this enterprise that Mr. Gisborne's company broke down, through failure of funds, and that, as we have seen, he transferred its interests to Mr. Cyrus W. Field.

In support of Mr. Gisborne's claims, I am permitted to cite the following letter from D. J. Henderson, Esq., of St. Johns, who was associated with Mr. Gisborne in the original enterprise : —

St. Johns, N.F., May 9, 1885.

Rev. M. Harvey : —

Rev. and dear Sir, — In compliance with your request to state what I know regarding Mr. F. N. Gisborne's claim to be the originator of the plan to connect Newfoundland with Ireland by a submarine cable, I beg to say that I was present at the first meeting held in Mr. Field's house, New York, at which Mr. Gisborne first unfolded his plans to Mr. Field and his friends.

This meeting took place about February 15th, 1854. I heard Mr. Gisborne, on this occasion, first explain his plan of connecting Newfoundland with the American continent; and he then unfolded a map on which he had traced the course of a submarine cable from Newfoundland to the coast of Ireland. Mr. Field at once remarked, in reference to the latter part of his project, " Ah, this puts a different complexion on the whole thing! "

It was this idea of uniting the two continents, by a cable across the bed of the Atlantic, which appeared forcibly to arrest the attention of Mr. Field, and to give the project its supreme value in his eyes. Mr. Gisborne distinctly outlined this plan, in my presence, to Mr. Field and his friends who were present, namely, Messrs. M. Taylor, M. O. Roberts, and C. White.

Yours very truly,
D. J. Henderson.

The following facts regarding the lengths of the principal submarine cables of the world are of interest. They are derived from the Dominion map projected by Mr. F. N. Gisborne, and published in 1883 : —

	Length in Knots.
First Atlantic cable, 1858	2,200
5 cables from Ireland to Newfoundland, average	1,870
From Newfoundland to Sydney, C.B., *via* Placentia Bay,	280

From Newfoundland to Sydney, *via* St. Pierre	300
From France to St. Pierre	2,584
From St. Pierre to Massachusetts	749
From England to Nova Scotia direct	2,540
From Nova Scotia to Massachusetts	500
Total cable distances from England to Australia, *via* India	10,334
Total cable distances from England to China, *via* India	9,879
Hong-Kong to Japan, *via* Shanghai	1,668
Total length of submarine cables laid up to 1883	60,000

PROJECTED LINES.

	Knots.
Total cable distance from England to China, *via* Canada	7,920
Hong-Kong, China, to New Guinea	2,000
New Guinea to Port Darwin, in Australia	800
Total cable distance from England to Australia, *via* Canada	10,780

APPENDIX II.

VALUE OF THE FISHERIES.

THE principal commercial fishes taken from the waters around Newfoundland and Labrador are the cod, the seal, the herring, the salmon, and the lobster. The cod-fishery is by far the most important, its products averaging in value three-fourths of the entire returns of the fisheries. If we take three years, ending in 1882, the total value of the codfish taken in that time was $18,102,728, so that the average annual value of the cod-fishery at present is $6,034,242. This calculation includes the dried codfish exported, the quantity consumed by the population, and the oil extracted from the fish.

FRENCH COD-FISHERIES.

The value of the codfish taken by the French on that portion of the coast of Newfoundland over which their fishing privileges extend is at present $279,436 per annum. In addition the French carry on the Bank fishery. In 1879 they had employed in the Bank and shore fishery 7,168 men, 177 vessels, of 27,865 tons, and the quantity of codfish taken was 369,628 quintals, the value of which was $1,342,544.

SEAL-FISHERY.

The average number of seals taken in three years, ending 1881, was 435,413; their annual average value was $1,026,896.

HERRING-FISHERY.

The chief centres of the herring-fishery are Labrador, St. George's Bay, Bay of Islands, Fortune Bay. The average annual value of the herrings exported and consumed in the country is $581,543.

SALMON-FISHERY.

The average annual value of the salmon exported is $114,505.

LOBSTER-FISHERY.

The annual average value of lobsters exported is at present $104,184.

The foregoing figures show that the total average value of all the fisheries is close on eight millions of dollars per annum.

NUMBER OF FISHERMEN.

According to the census of 1873 there were 45,845 persons employed in fishing and curing fish. At present that number has increased to about 54,000.

In 1874 the number of able-bodied fishermen in the colony was 26,377; at present they number about 33,000.

APPENDIX III.

AGRICULTURAL RESOURCES.

THE best answer to the assertion, so often repeated, that the soil of Newfoundland is unfit for cultivation, is that, even on the limited and imperfect system now pursued, the average annual value of agricultural products is $612,350; and the value of the land now under cultivation, together with the cattle, sheep, and horses, is $2,500,000.

The geological survey has shown that in the regions near and surrounding St. George's Bay, including the Codroy valleys, there are 730 square miles suitable for settlement. Bay of Islands, including the valley of the Humber, Deer Lake, and Grand Lake, contains 630 square miles suitable for settlement. These valleys are, for the most part, covered with valuable timber. In the Gander, Gambo, and Terra-Nova valleys there are 1,700 square miles available for settlement. The Exploits valley and Red Indian Lake, with the lands surrounding the estuary of the Exploits, contain 1,620 square miles. Thus, in these great valleys alone, we have 4,650 square miles, or 2,976,000 acres, fit for settlement, and capable, when cultivated, of sustaining in comfort a large population.

In addition to these large and extensive tracts there are many smaller portions of excellent soil around the heads of the bays, along the margins of the smaller rivers, and on several of the islands. When we add to these the land already under culture around the various settlements, and the wide area in the peninsula of Avalon, which is admirably adapted for cattle and sheep raising, we have 2,000,000 acres more; or, in all, 5,000,000 acres fitted for agricultural and grazing purposes. What the interior proper may contain is yet unknown.

FORESTS.

The chief varieties of forest timber are white-pine, white and black spruce, tamarack or larch, fir, yellow and white birch. In the Gander districts alone there are, according to the geological survey, 850 square miles of pine lands, or, including some of the neighbouring regions, a total area of 1,000 square miles. Mr. Murray pronounces this a splendid lumbering region. where an immense timber trade could be successfully carried on. Groves of pine are occasionally found here in which the average girth of trees is nine feet, and many individual trees reach twelve and even fourteen feet. Other timber regions are the valley of the Exploits, Red Indian Lake, the valley of the Humber, and the valleys around St. George's Bay, and in the Codroy district. The soil in these districts, when cleared, will yield cereal and other crops in abundance.

APPENDIX IV.

MINERAL RESOURCES.

So far as explorations and mining operations have gone Newfoundland ranks high among the copper-producing countries of the world. The chief seat of copper-mining is around the shores of Notre Dame Bay. The ore is found in connection with the serpentine rocks, and these rocks are spread over an area of 5,000 square miles, most of which is yet unexplored. Up to 1879 the value of copper and nickel ore exported was $4,629,889, or nearly £1,000,000 sterling. Gold has been found, but as yet only in small quantities. Rich deposits of lead-ore have also been found in several places, especially at Port-a-Port. Gypsum is found in immense developments, and marbles on both eastern and western shores. Roofing-slate is another valuable material found in abundance. The coal area of St. George's Bay is 25 miles wide by 10 in length.

APPENDIX V.

GOVERNMENT.

The form of government consists of a Governor, who is appointed by the crown, and whose term of office is usually about six years; an Executive Council, representing the party commanding a majority in the Legislature, and consisting of seven members; a Legislative Council, or Upper House, of fifteen members, nominated by the Governor in Council, and holding office for life; and a House of Assembly, of thirty-three members, elected every four years by the votes of the people. The seventeen electoral districts, sending thirty-three members, are divided as follows:—

	Members.
St. John's, East	3
St. John's, West	3
Harbour Grace	2
Carbonear	1
Harbour Maine	2
Port de Grave	1
Bay de Verds	1
Trinity	3
Bonavista	3
Twillingate and Fogo	3
Ferryland	2
Placentia and St. Mary's	3
Burin	2
Fortune Bay	1
Burgeo and La Poile	1
St. George	1
St. Barbe	1

An Act of the Legislature, passed in the session of 1885, gives one additional member to each of the three districts of Harbour Grace, Bay de Verds, and Twillingate and Fogo, in consequence of the increase in their population as shown by the Census of 1884. The House of Assembly will in future consist of 36 members.

The right of voting is conferred on every man who for one year immediately preceding the day of election has occupied a dwelling-house within the island, either as owner or tenant.

The Supreme Court is composed of a Chief-Justice and two assistant judges, appointed by the crown. The Court of Labrador has civil and criminal jurisdiction over such parts of Labrador as lie within the government of Newfoundland. It is presided over by one judge, who is appointed by the Governor in Council.

APPENDIX VI.

EDUCATION.

The interest in education is deepening and extending. A liberal provision is made for it by the Legislature, amounting now to $93,952 per annum. The improvements already secured afford sufficient guarantees of future progress. Each religious denomination receives a grant for education from the public funds in proportion to its numbers. Separate Boards of Education in the different districts have charge of the schools. Three superintendents are appointed by Government, — one for Roman Catholic schools, one for Church of England, and one for Wesleyan schools.

In 1881 there were in all 416 elementary schools. Of these 157 belonged to the Church of England, 158 to the Roman Catholics, 99 to the Methodists, and 2 to the Congregationalists. The total number of pupils in the elementary schools was 24,292.

"The Colonial and Continental Church Society," originally "The Newfoundland School Society," has done much for the cause of education in Newfoundland. It commenced operations in 1823, and may be said to have initiated common-school education in the island. It has still 20 schools in operation, attended by 2,295 scholars. Its central school, in St. John's, is largely attended, and is used by the Church of England Boards of Education as a training-school for their teachers, male and female, twenty teachers being sent out every year.

The Christian Brothers have in operation a school in St. John's, attended by about 400 pupils. The school-rooms are admirably arranged and equipped; the instruction imparted is deservedly spoken of in the highest terms, and an excellent educational work is carried on.

The academies and grammar schools are attended by 674 pupils. There are but two grammar schools. — one in Harbour Grace and one in Carbonear. — both of which are well conducted, and have rendered, and continue to render, good service to the cause of education. The four academies are in St. John's, and are conducted on the denominational principle. They are well-managed, efficient institutions, having each a full staff of competent teachers, and imparting a superior education. All of them prepare pupils for the universities. St. John's has lately been made a centre of the London University, and already two pupils from the Roman Catholic Academy, or St. Bonaventure College, and two from the Wesleyan Academy, have passed the matriculation examinations with much credit.

APPENDIX VII.

RELIGIOUS DENOMINATIONS.

CHURCH OF ENGLAND.

" The Society for the Propagation of the Gospel in Foreign Parts " first sent a missionary to Newfoundland in 1703. In 1787 the first colonial bishopric was created, — that of Nova Scotia, to which Newfoundland was attached. It was not, however, till 1827 that Bishop Inglis, of Nova Scotia, was able to visit this portion of his extensive diocese. He found but 9 clergymen and missionaries in the whole island. In 1839 Newfoundland and the Bermudas were erected into a separate diocese, and the Rev. Aubrey S. Spencer was appointed Bishop of the new See. In 1844 Bishop Spencer was succeeded by Dr. Edward Feild, of Queen's College, Oxford, who continued Bishop till his death, in 1876. His successor was Dr. J. B. Kelly, who was compelled by failing health to resign, in 1877. In 1878 he was succeeded by the Rev. Llewellyn Jones, D.D., who is now Bishop of the diocese.

The diocese is now divided into 8 deaneries, and the number of clergy is 50. The total number of churches in Newfoundland and Labrador is 102.

ROMAN CATHOLIC CHURCH.

The Roman Catholic Church in Newfoundland was first publicly organized in 1784, by the appointment of Dr. O'Donnell, as Prefect Apostolic, by Pope Pius VI. In 1796 Dr. O'Donnell was appointed Vicar Apostolic and Bishop. In 1807 he was succeeded by Dr. Patrick Lambert, who held office till 1817, when Dr. Thomas Scallan was appointed Bishop. He died in 1830, and was succeeded by Bishop Fleming, who held office till 1850, when Dr. Mullock was appointed as his successor. He held office till his death, in 1869, and in 1870 the present bishop, the Rt. Rev. Thomas Joseph Power, was consecrated, in Rome, by His Eminence Cardinal Cullen. In 1856 Newfoundland was divided into two dioceses, St. John's and Harbour Grace, Dr. Dalton being the first Bishop of the latter; and his successors were Rev. Henry Carfagnini, and Dr. Macdonald, who is the present Bishop. In the St. John's diocese there are now a cathedral, 26 churches, besides chapels, 29 priests, a college, 13 convents, and a female orphanage. In the diocese of Harbour Grace there are a cathedral, 14 churches, besides chapels, 16 priests, and 5 convents. In the prefecture apostolic of St. George, West Newfoundland, there are 3 churches and 3 priests.

WESLEYAN METHODISM.

The Rev. Lawrence Coghlan was the first Wesleyan missionary, in 1765. In 1814 Newfoundland was constituted a separate district, with a superintendent. In 1840 there were 14 ministers and 10 local preachers. At present Newfoundland is constituted a separate conference, with a president, and is divided into 3 districts, — St. John's, Carbonear, and Bonavista. The total number of ministers is 49; of churches, 44.

CONGREGATIONALISM.

Congregationalism dates from 1775. In 1779 the Rev. John Jones was ordained in England to be minister of a church in St. John's. There are now two additional Congregational churches, — one at Twillingate and one at Rendell Harbour, and two mission stations at Fortune Bay.

PRESBYTERIANISM.

The first Presbyterian church was organized in 1842, of which the Rev. Donald A. Fraser was minister. A Free Church Presbyterian congregation was formed in 1848, in St. John's, and a second, in Harbour Grace, in 1855. The two congregations in St. John's united in 1877, and built St. Andrew's Church. There is a Presbyterian mission station at Bay of Islands, and another at Little Bay Mine.

APPENDIX VIII.

POPULATION.

The earliest estimate of the resident population of the island was made in 1654, when it was ascertained that there were 350 families, in 15 different settlements, numbering about 1,750 persons. In 1698 the population was 2,640. In 1763 the population was 7,080; in 1785, 10,000; in 1804, 20,000; in 1825, 55,719; in 1832, 60,000; in 1836, 75,094; in 1845, 98,703; in 1857, 124,288; in 1869, 146,536; in 1874, 161,374. The

The census of 1874 gave the numerical strength of the different religious denominations as follows :—

Roman Catholics	64,317
Church of England	59,561
Wesleyans	35,702
Presbyterians	1,168
Congregationalists	461
Baptists and others	165

The following is an abstract of the census taken in 1884. It will be seen from it that the increase during the last decade has been 36,209 or 22.43 per cent. As the immigration during that period has been very small, and has probably been more than counterbalanced by the emigration, the increase shown by the recent census has been solely from natural causes, and proves that the people are in a healthy and fairly prosperous condition. Few countries have a normal rate of increase so high as Newfoundland.

Abstract of Census of 1874.

Districts.	Total.	Church of England.	Roman Catholic.	Methodist.	Others.
St. John's East	17,811	3,985	11,200	1,838	788
St. John's West	12,763	2,551	8,746	1,088	378
Harbour Main	7,174	1,716	5,361	97	
Port-de-Grave	7,919	3,415	2,002	2,501	1
Harbour Grace	13,055	7,239	4,013	1,615	188
Carbonear	5,488	939	2,189	2,362	8
Bay-de-Verds	7,434	439	1,775	5,220	
Trinity Bay	15,677	8,417	1,583	5,663	14
Bonavista	13,008	6,860	2,599	3,531	18
Twillingate and Fogo	15,135	6,989	1,956	6,172	18
Ferryland	6,419	173	6,246		
Placentia	9,857	1,351	8,254	239	13
Burin	7,678	1,633	2,689	3,351	5
Fortune	5,788	4,391	1,387	8	2
Burgeo and La Poile	5,098	4,216	125	731	26
[1] St. George's and St. Barbe	8,654	3,768	3,716	991	179
Total	158,958	58,072	63,841	35,407	1,638
Labrador	2,422	1,489	476	295	162
Total	161,380	59,561	64,317	35,702	1,800

[1] In 1874 St. George's and St. Barbe were not separate districts, and, for comparison, their population is also united in the table for 1884. St. George's has a total population of 5,535, of which 3,393 is Roman Catholic, 1,878 Church of England, 147 Methodist. St. Barbe has a total population of 6,498, of which 2,910 is Church of England, 1,639 Methodist, 1,872 Roman Catholic.

Abstract of Census of 1884.

Districts.	Total.	Increase	Church of England.	Increase	Roman Catholic.	Increase	Methodist.	Increase	Others.	Increase
St. John's East	21,840	4,029	5,089	1,104	13,269	2,069	2,463	625	1,019	231
St. John's West	16,297	3,534	3,207	636	10,509	1,763	2,023	935	558	180
Harbour Main	8,916	1,742	1,956	240	6,820	1,459	132	35	8	8
Port-de-Grave	8,685	766	†3,731	316	2,206	204	2,746	245	2	1
Harbour Grace	14,717	1,662	8,632	1,393	3,942	*71	1,948	333	195	7
Carbonear	6,224	736	1,029	100	2,262	73	2,920	558	13	5
Bay-de-Verds	8,403	969	430	*9	1,951	176	6,022	802		
Trinity Bay	19,005	3,328	†9,876	1,459	1,754	171	7,298	1,635	77	63
Bonavista	16,482	3,474	8,381	1,521	2,979	380	5,101	1,570	21	3
Twillingate and Fogo	20,289	5,154	6,775	*214	3,132	1,176	10,232	4,060	150	132
Ferryland	6,470	51	151	*22	6,316	70			3	3
Placentia	11,833	1,976	1,544	193	9,916	1,662	363	124	10	*3
Burin	8,726	1,018	1,798	165	2,684	*5	4,243	892	1	*4
Fortune	6,914	1,126	5,166	775	1,607	220	36	28	105	103
Burgeo and La Poile	6,544	1,446	5,119	903	152	27	1,265	534	8	*18
‡St. George's and St. Barbe	12,033	3,379	4,788	1,020	5,265	1,549	1,846	855	134	*45
Total	193,378	34,420	67,672	9,600	74,764	10,925	48,638	13,231	2,304	666
Labrador	4,211	1,789	1,974	485	566	90	305	10	1,366	1,204
Total	197,589	36,209	69,646	10,085	75,330	11,015	48,943	13,241	3,670	1,870

‡ In 1874 St. George's and St. Barbe were not separate districts, and, for comparison, their population is also united in the table for 1884. St. George's has a total population of 5,535, of which 3,393 is Roman Catholic, 1,878 Church of England, 147 Methodist. St. Barbe has a total population of 6,498, of which 2,910 is Church of England, 1,639 Methodist, 1,872 Roman Catholic.

* The Church of England decreased 9 in Bay-de-Verds, 214 in Twillingate and Fogo, and 22 in Ferryland. The Church of Rome decreased 71 in Harbour Grace, and 5 in Burin. † In Port-de-Grave there are 401 members of the Reformed Church, and in Trinity there are 222, and for convenience these have been included with the members of the Church of England.

APPENDIX IX.

REVENUE, IMPORTS, AND EXPORTS.

In 1880 the revenue was $897,474; in 1881, $1,003,803; in 1882, $1,119,385; in 1883, $1,251,987; in 1884, $1,170,602.

The exports in 1881 were, in value, $7,648,574; in 1882, $8,228,291; in 1883, $7,996,795; in 1884, $9,061,186.

The imports in 1880 were, in value, $6,966,243; in 1881, $6,863,708; in 1883, $9,181,464.

The public debt in 1881 was $1,351,008, or about $7 *per capita*. A sinking-fund has been established for its liquidation.

APPENDIX X.

LIST OF PREMIERS UNDER RESPONSIBLE GOVERNMENT.

1854. — Hon. Philip Francis Little.
1858. — Hon. John Kent.
1861. — Hon. Hugh Hoyles (afterwards Sir Hugh).
1865. — Hon. F. B. T. Carter (afterwards Sir F. B. T.).
1869. — Hon C. F. Bennett.
1873. — Hon. F. B. T. Carter.
1878. — Hon. W. V. Whiteway (afterwards Sir William Vallance Whiteway).
1882. — Sir William V. Whiteway.
1885. — Sir William V. Whiteway

APPENDIX XI.

LIST OF GOVERNORS OF NEWFOUNDLAND.

Appointed.

1729. — Captain Henry Osborne, R.N.
1731. — Captain Clinton.
1734. — Captain Lord Viscount Muskery.
1737. — Captain Vanburg.
1740. — Captain Right Hon. Lord George Graham.
1741. — Captain Hon. John Byng.
1744. — Captain Sir Charles Hardy.
1749. — Captain Lord George Brydges Rodney.
1750. — Captain Francis H. Drake.
1753. — Captain Bonfoy.
1755. — Captain Dorril.
1757. — Captain Edwards.
1760. — Captain Webb.
1761. — Captain Lord Graves.
1764. — Captain Palliser.
1769. — Captain Hon. John Byron.
1772. — Commodore Molyneux, afterwards Lord Shuldham.
1775. — Commodore Duff.
1776. — Rear-Admiral Montague.
1779. — Rear-Admiral Edwards.
1782. — Vice-Admiral John Campbell.
1786. — Rear-Admiral Elliot.
1789. — Admiral Mark Milbanke.
1792. — Admiral King.
1794. — Admiral Sir James Wallace.
1797. — Vice-Admiral Waldegrave.
1800. — Vice-Admiral Pole.

Appointed.

1802. — Admiral Lord Gambier.
1804. — Admiral Sir Erasmus Gower.
1807. — Admiral Holloway.
1810. — Vice-Admiral Sir Thomas Duckworth.
1813. — Vice-Admiral Sir Richard G. Keates.
1816. — Vice-Admiral Pickmore.
1818. — Captain Bowker (Administrator).
1818. — Admiral Sir Charles Hamilton.
1825. — Captain Sir Thomas Cochrane.
1834. — Captain Henry Prescott.
1841. — Major-General Sir John Harvey.
1846. — Lieutenant-Colonel Law (Administrator).
1847. — Sir John Gaspard Le Marchant.
1852. — Hon. James Crowdy (Administrator).
1852. — Ker Baillie Hamilton.
1857. — Hon. Lawrence O'Brien (Administrator).
1857. — Sir Alexander Bannerman.
1864. — Hon. Lawrence O'Brien (Administrator).
1864. — Anthony Musgrave.
1869. — Sir Stephen J. Hill, K.C.M.G., C.B.
1876. — Sir John Hawley Glover, K.C.M.G.
1880. — Sir Fred. B. T. Carter (Administrator).
1881. — Sir Henry Fitzhardinge B. Maxse.
1883. — Hon. Edward Morris (Administrator).
1883. — Sir Fred. B. T. Carter (Administrator).
1884. — Sir John H. Glover, K.C.M.G.

BY THE SAME AUTHOR,

PRICE EIGHTEEN SHILLINGS STERLING,

NEWFOUNDLAND,

THE OLDEST BRITISH COLONY.

LONDON: CHAPMAN AND HALL, 1883.

American Edition, Revised and Enlarged.

BOSTON: DOYLE & WHITTLE, 1883.

450 Pages. Price $2.50.

MAP AND ILLUSTRATIONS.

Opinions of the English Press.

(From the Fortnightly Review.)

This work on Newfoundland is a difficult task, extremely well executed. Take it all in all it is an admirable account of the oldest English Colony, plainly written, pleasantly illustrated, and unique as the best, as it is undoubtedly the most recent work on the country.

(From the London Academy.)

A section is devoted to the interesting history of Newfoundland, the battles of the early settlers for their freedom, their patient loyalty under many provocations to a contrary course, the attempt to make it a mere fishing station. But the section to which the reader will turn with most zest is that on the fisheries. In no other work is the Newfoundland staple trade treated so fully and so well; and these chapters alone would give the volume a lasting value. The physical geography of the country is amply described. The ethnology is excellent, and the meteorological remarks are useful. It is an admirable book, worthy of soon attaining the second edition, which will give the writer an opportunity of still further improving it. It is illustrated with some spirited wood-cuts.

(From the Pall Mall Gazette.)

An interesting and well-written work. . . . . Mr. Harvey is eminently qualified, by long residence and scientific attainments, for the collection of local details and statistics; and even those who are not personally interested in the future of the colony will find much to please and instruct them in his descriptions of the aborigines, the scenery, the fisheries, and, above all, the gigantic cuttle-fish, which he was the first to rescue from the domain of romance and introduce into the domain of authentic natural history.

(From the London Graphic.)

A volume which is not only very readable, but one to be set aside after reading as a standard work of reference on the resources of a somewhat neglected country.

PRESS NOTICES.

(From the London Spectator.)

If the general public will read this interesting book about that despised country it will clear up their hazy notions in a very surprising and agreeable manner. . . . . The descriptions are very clear and interesting, and the chapters on seal-fishing are among the very best parts of the book. . . . . With these short extracts we will take our leave of a most entertaining and useful book, which we hope will find a great many readers both in England and in Newfoundland.

(From the St. James's Gazette.)

A complete and graphic account of the discovery, at the close of the fifteenth century, of what is now the oldest dependency of England; and its history and progress are traced through nearly four hundred years. . . . . The Newfoundlanders seem now to be fairly on the high road to that prosperity which was so long denied them, and which this interesting book shows that they merit.

(From Land and Water.)

The story of Newfoundland constitutes one of the most interesting chapters in the history of the New World. It is told so attractively and completely that we doubt if it will ever require retelling. It may be supplemented, but not superseded.

(From the European Mail.)

No more interesting work has ever come under our notice than this. . . . . We may add that it is highly instructive, full of eloquent and graphic description, and teeming with historical facts and useful statistical information hitherto beyond the reach of the general public. There is a handy and useful index, and some capital illustrations.

(From the London Daily Telegraph.)

This volume is composed in a very hopeful spirit as to the future of the colony, and is well calculated to interest its readers in a country which possesses much natural beauty and great unexplored and undeveloped resources.

(From the Scotsman.)

The book is a piece of solid workmanship. It traces not only the history of the foundation and progress of the colony, but enters fully into the physical geography and topography of Newfoundland, its agricultural, mining, and fishing resources.

(From the London Daily News.)

The work leaves no part of the field unexplored, even the political and financial affairs of the island being treated in some detail. Altogether, this is not only a work of interest to the general reader, but by far the most complete account of Newfoundland that has yet appeared.

(From the London Standard.)

The cod-fisheries of Newfoundland are almost worthy of a book to themselves; and when we add to them the seal-hunting, the salmon and caribou and ptarmigan, leading us from trade to sport, and showing us the capabilities of this great island, we are led into something like enthusiasm about the great and unknown estate long held by us. . . . . The book is one to be recommended to all readers.

(From London Society.)

We can heartily recommend this handsome and exhaustive volume, recently published by Messrs. Chapman and Hall.

(From Figaro.)

The book has many merits which will commend it to the reading public. It is not only free from the cardinal vice of dulness, but is instructive and, in many respects, entertaining.

(From the Literary World.)

An exceedingly interesting and valuable book. It is illustrated with photographs and sketches made for the work, which give it great interest and value.

(From the London Mining Journal.)

An interesting and useful volume.

(From the Birmingham Daily Post.)

A handsome volume of more than 500 pages, liberally and admirably illustrated, — a remarkably readable work. . . . . The chapter on the fisheries is one of the most valuable and original in the volume. Even more interesting is the seal-fishery, of which so little has hitherto been known. These chapters alone will make this volume very welcome to all readers, as an original and brilliant description of the great fisheries of the world.

(From the Leeds Mercury.)

The work is eminently readable, the style being easy and the selection of material judicious. It is rendered the more attractive by a series of illustrations. The work, indeed, leaves little to be desired.

(From the Nottingham Guardian.)

A very valuable contribution to the literature of our oldest colony. The work will, we have no doubt, live long. It will be some time before any other writers venture to tread in the footsteps of the present writer.

Opinions of the American and Colonial Press.

(From the Atlantic Monthly.)

An interesting work by a painstaking student, who sets about a thorough representation of the country.

(From the New York Herald.)

The best account of Newfoundland ever printed.

(From the New York Evening Post.)

The book is indeed good and interesting, and well-written, but is without the smallest bit of imagination or fancy to mislead the reader. It is no Sir John Mandeville's tale of things seen golden-purplish and out of shape through an ill-fitted spy-glass. It has in it all the earnestness of conviction and of faith in the holding of strong facts. The book does not make the strangeness of the story. The book only puts the case to the world of readers in a plain unvarnished way, in good English, and with good sense, and proves it and makes it clear by ample testimony and figures.

(From the Republic, Boston.)

The historical part of the work has been not only well done, but is highly creditable for its broad, liberal, and comprehensive grasp of religious and political events, in which the temptations to become partisan have been admirably avoided. . . . As a book of reference, "Newfoundland" will be found simply invaluable. It is profusely and capitally illustrated, elegantly printed, and neatly and serviceably bound.

(From the Wheelman.)

It is, we must confess, one of the most fascinating histories we ever read.

(From the Boston Transcript.)

There is a fine unity in the work; it reveals no awkward seams, and the whole is absorbingly interesting.

PRESS NOTICES.

(From the Boston Saturday Evening Gazette.)

It is the most important work hitherto published about Newfoundland. The materials have been gathered for the most part on the spot, and every publication dealing with the subject has been carefully studied and utilized, together with all public records and other documents.

(From the Boston Post.)

It is the only thorough, comprehensive, and reliable work upon the great island that has ever been published.

(From the Cincinnati Gazette.)

It is a complete and very creditable work.

(From the Boston Pilot.)

The republication of the book in this country is timely, and we bespeak for it a hearty recognition.

(From the Toronto Globe.)

It is one of the most valuable additions to the literature of the British colonies which has ever appeared. The Rev. Mr. Harvey is a recognized authority on all matters connected with Newfoundland. He has resided there for more than a quarter of a century, and no man living is more intimately acquainted with its history, resources, and possibilities. His letters to the "Globe," some years ago, will be long remembered. They were a revelation to all classes in the community. To most of us he was, in a very real sense, the discoverer of Newfoundland. The book has already attained well-merited popularity.

(From the Montreal Gazette.)

The Rev. M. Harvey, having been for many years our Newfoundland correspondent, will require but few words of introduction from us. His letters to this journal have been admired and enjoyed by hundreds of readers, as well for the valuable information of which they were full, as for the clear and systematic manner in which the writer dealt with all objects that occupied his attention. We are simply stating the truth when we say, that there is no one living could be better fitted by his wide and intimate knowledge of the country, its people, and resources, as well as by judgment, taste, and ability as a writer, to contribute to a work of this kind than he is. . . . The history is an exceedingly well-told story. The other sections of the work are of no less interest. No one who desires to know the truth about Newfoundland, its capabilities and prospects should fail to secure a copy.

(From the Quebec Morning Chronicle.)

It is one of the most instructive and interesting books that the press of England has given us for a long time. . . . It will do for Newfoundland what "Wallace's Russia" has done for that vast empire, and what "Dent's Last Forty Years" has done for Canada. Every chapter reveals a monument of labour on the part of the author. No pains have been spared, evidently, to secure accuracy in every detail. We can cordially commend this valuable book to our readers.

(From the Halifax Morning Chronicle.)

The whole work is as interesting as a novel, and all who wish to become conversant with "Ye Antient Colonye" of Newfoundland should possess themselves of a copy of this able and instructive work, of which the above is but an imperfect and meagre description.

(From the Newfoundlander.)

It is no disparagement of the labours of earlier authorities to say that, in point of general usefulness at the present day, they are quite surpassed by the volume now before us. . . . It comes out at a most opportune period; and all who seek to form just opinions of the past, present, and future of the colony should possess a volume which is not less inviting in its external get-up, than in the literary impress stamped upon its pages.

www.ingramcontent.com/pod-product-compliance
Lightning Source LLC
Chambersburg PA
CBHW021727220426
43662CB00008B/746